Trevor Baker, Neil Dixon and Bob Woo

ESSENTIALS

OCR GCSE

Additional Science A

Ideas about Science

The OCR Twenty First Century Additional Science specification aims to ensure that you develop an **understanding of science itself** – of how scientific knowledge is obtained, the kinds of evidence and reasoning behind it, its strengths and limitations, and how far we can rely on it.

These issues are explored through Ideas about Science, which are built into the specification content and summarised over the following pages.

The tables below give an overview of the Ideas about Science that can be assessed in each unit and provide examples of content which support them in this guide.

Unit A162 (Modules B4, B5 and B6)

Ideas about Science	Example of Supporting Content
Data: their importance and limitations	Collecting Data about how Light Affects Plants (page 10)
Cause–effect explanations	Limiting Factors for Photosynthesis (page 9)
Developing scientific explanations	Memory (page 30)
Making decisions about science and technology	Stem Cells (page 18)

Unit A172 (Modules C4, C5 and C6)

Ideas about Science	Example of Supporting Content
Data: their importance and limitations	Collecting Titration Data (page 63)
Cause–effect explanations	Collision Theory (page 65)
Developing scientific explanations	Properties of Ionic Compounds (page 48)
The scientific community	The Development of the Periodic Table (page 35)
Risk	Hazardous Substances (page 38)
Making decisions about science and technology	Metals and the Environment (page 52)

Unit A182 (Modules P4, P5 and P6)

Ideas about Science	Example of Supporting Content
Data: their importance and limitations	Measuring the Half-life (page 94)
Cause–effect explanations	Background Radiation (page 93)
Developing scientific explanations	Alpha Particle Scattering Experiment (page 98)
Risk	Uses of Radiation (page 95)
Making decisions about science and technology	Nuclear Waste (page 96)

Data: Their Importance and Limitations

Science is built on **data**. Scientists carry out experiments to collect and interpret data, seeing whether the data agree with their explanations. If the data do agree, then it means the current explanation is more likely to be correct. If not, then the explanation has to be changed.

Experiments aim to find out what the **'true'** value of a quantity is. Quantities are affected by **errors** made when carrying out the experiment and **random variation**. This means that the measured value may be different to the true value. Scientists try to **control** all the factors that could cause this uncertainty.

Scientists always take **repeat readings** to try to make sure that they have accurately estimated the true value of a quantity. The **mean** is calculated and is the best estimate of what the true value of a quantity is. The more times an experiment is repeated, the greater the chance that the mean value will be very close to the true value.

The **range**, or spread, of data gives an indication of where the true value must lie. Sometimes a measurement will not be in the zone where the majority of readings fall. It may look like the result (called an **'outlier'**) is wrong – however, it doesn't automatically mean that it is. The outlier has to be checked by repeating the measurement of that quantity. If the result can't be checked, then it should still be used.

Here is an example of an outlier in a set of data:

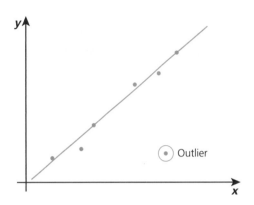

Outlier

(HT) The spread of the data around the mean (the range) gives an idea of whether it really is different to the mean from another measurement. If the ranges for each mean don't overlap, then it's more likely that the two means are different. However, sometimes the ranges do overlap and there may be no significant difference between them.

The ranges also give an indication of reliability – a wide range makes it more difficult to say with certainty that the true value of a quantity has been measured. A small range suggests that the mean is closer to the true value.

If an outlier is discovered, you need to be able to defend your decision as to whether you keep it or discard it.

Ideas about Science

Cause-Effect Explanations

Science is based on the idea that a factor has an effect on an outcome. Scientists make **predictions** as to how the **input variable** will change the **outcome variable**. To make sure that only the input variable can affect the outcome, scientists try to control all the other variables that could potentially alter it. This is called '**fair testing**'.

You need to be able to explain why it's necessary to control all the factors that might affect the outcome. This means suggesting how they could influence the outcome of the experiment.

A **correlation** is where there's an apparent link between a factor and an outcome. It may be that as the factor increases, the outcome increases as well. On the other hand, it may be that when the factor increases, the outcome decreases.

For example, there's a correlation between temperature and the rate of rusting – the higher the temperature, the more rapid the rate of rusting.

Just because there's a correlation doesn't necessarily mean that the factor causes the outcome. Further experiments are needed to establish this. It could be that another factor causes the outcome or that both the original factor and outcome are caused by something else.

The following graph suggests a correlation between going to the opera regularly and living longer. It's far more likely that if you have the money to go to the opera, you can afford a better diet and health care. Going to the opera isn't the true cause of the correlation.

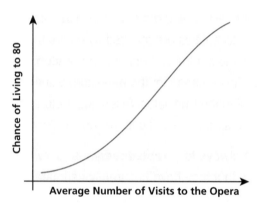

Sometimes the factor may alter the chance of an outcome occurring but doesn't guarantee it will lead to it. The statement 'the more time spent on a sun bed the greater the chance of developing skin cancer' is an example of this type of correlation, as some people will not develop skin cancer even if they do spend a lot of time on a sun bed.

To investigate the link between one **variable** and another variable, scientists have to try to ensure that all other variables are adequately **controlled**. They also have to repeat the experiment and ideally they investigate the link between the variables in other situations and reactions as well. If the link is the same, no matter what reaction is being studied, scientists can be confident about the conclusions they've made about cause and effect.

HT Even so, a correlation and cause will still not be accepted by scientists unless there's a scientific mechanism that can explain them.

Developing Scientific Explanations

Scientists devise **hypotheses** (predictions of what will happen in an experiment), along with an **explanation** (the scientific mechanism behind the hypotheses) and **theories** (that can be tested).

Explanations involve thinking creatively to work out why data have a particular pattern. Good scientific explanations account for most or all of the data already known. Sometimes they may explain a range of phenomena that weren't previously thought to be linked. Explanations should enable predictions to be made about new situations or examples.

When deciding on which is the better of two explanations, you should be able to give reasons why.

Explanations are tested by comparing predictions based on them with data from observations or experiments. If there's an agreement between the experimental findings, then it increases the chance of the explanation being right. However, it doesn't prove it's correct. Likewise, if the prediction and observation indicate that one or the other is wrong, it decreases the confidence in the explanation on which the prediction is based.

The Scientific Community

Once a scientist has carried out enough experiments to back up his/her claims, they have to be reported. This enables the **scientific community** to carefully check the claims, something which is required before they're accepted as scientific knowledge.

Scientists attend **conferences** where they share their findings and sound out new ideas and explanations. This can lead to scientists revisiting their work or developing links with other laboratories to improve it.

The next step is writing a formal **scientific paper** and submitting it to a **journal** in the relevant field. The paper is allocated to **peer reviewers** (experts in their field), who carefully check and evaluate the paper. If the peer reviewers accept the paper, then it's published. Scientists then read the paper and check the work themselves.

New scientific claims that haven't been evaluated by the whole scientific community have less credibility than well-established claims.

It takes time for other scientists to gather enough evidence that a theory is sound. If the results can't be repeated or replicated by themselves or others, then scientists will be sceptical about the new claims.

If the explanations can't be arrived at from the available data, then it's fair and reasonable for different scientists to come up with alternative explanations. These will be based on the background and experience of the scientists. It's through further experimentation that the best explanation will be chosen.

This means that the current explanation has the greatest support. New data aren't enough to topple it. Only when the new data are sufficiently repeated and checked will the original explanation be changed.

(HT) You need to be able to suggest reasons why an accepted explanation will not be given up immediately when new data, which appear to conflict with it, have been published.

Ideas about Science

Risk

Everything we do (or not do) carries **risk**. Nothing is completely risk-free. New technologies and processes based on scientific advances often introduce new risks.

Risk is sometimes calculated by measuring the chance of something occurring in a large sample over a given period of time (**calculated risk**). This enables people to take informed decisions about whether the risk is worth taking. In order to decide, you have to balance the **benefit** (to individuals or groups) with the **consequences** of what could happen. For example, deciding whether or not to add chlorine to drinking water involves weighing up the benefit (of reducing the spread of cholera) against the risk (of a toxic chlorine leak at the purification plant).

Risk which is associated with something that someone has chosen to do is easier to accept than risk which has been imposed on them. Individuals might also be more willing to accept risks that have short-term effects rather than long-term ones.

HT Perception of risk changes depending on our personal experience (**perceived risk**). Familiar risks (e.g. using bleach without wearing gloves) tend to be under-estimated, whilst unfamiliar risks (e.g. making chlorine in the laboratory) and invisible or long-term risks (e.g. cleaning up mercury from a broken thermometer) tend to be over-estimated.

For example, many people under-estimate the risk that adding limescale remover and bleach to a toilet at the same time might produce toxic chlorine gas.

Governments and public bodies try to assess risk and create **policy** on what is and what isn't acceptable. This can be controversial, especially when the people who benefit most aren't the ones at risk.

Making Decisions about Science and Technology

Science has helped to create new technologies that have improved the world, benefiting millions of people. However, there can be unintended **consequences** of new technologies, even many decades after they were first introduced. These could be related to the impact on the environment or to the quality of life.

When introducing new technologies, the potential benefits must be weighed up against the risks. Sometimes unintended consequences affecting the environment can be identified. By applying the scientific method (making hypotheses, explanations and carrying out experiments), scientists can devise new ways of putting right the impact. Devising **life cycle assessments** helps scientists to try to minimise unintended consequences and ensure sustainability.

Some areas of science could have a high potential risk to individuals or groups if they go wrong or if they're abused. In these areas the Government ensures that regulations are in place.

The scientific approach covers anything where data can be collected and used to test a hypothesis. It can't be used when evidence can't be collected (e.g. it can't test beliefs or values).

Just because something can be done doesn't mean that it should be done. Some areas of scientific research or the technologies resulting from them have **ethical issues** associated with them. This means that not all people will necessarily agree with it.

Ethical decisions have to be made, taking into account the views of everyone involved, whilst balancing the benefits and risks. It's impossible to please everybody, so decisions are often made on the basis of which outcome will benefit most people. Within a culture there will also be some actions that are always right or wrong, no matter what the circumstances are.

These sample questions and model answers will help you to prepare for aspects of Ideas about Science in your exam. Some of the exam practice questions in this guide (e.g. questions 3 and 4 on page 33) will also help you to prepare for these types of question.

1. Many people are worried about global warming but there are still some politicians who deny that carbon dioxide produced by human activity is causing global warming. The graph shows how the amount of carbon dioxide in the atmosphere on a remote island in the Pacific Ocean has changed. It also shows how mean air temperature has changed.

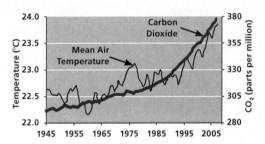

(a) Describe the correlation between the amount of carbon dioxide in the atmosphere and the mean air temperature. [1]

As the amount of carbon dioxide increased, so did the mean air temperature.

(b) The politicians who do not believe in global warming say that this correlation does not prove a cause-and-effect link between carbon dioxide and global warming. Explain the difference between correlation and cause-and-effect. Use the graph to illustrate your answer. [6]

✏ *The quality of written communication will be assessed in your answer to this question.*

A correlation is when a change in the measured factor (outcome variable) occurs at the same time as a change in another factor (input variable). The graph shows that the rise in air temperature happened at the same time and at a similar rate to the increase in carbon dioxide. However, correlation doesn't necessarily indicate a causal link. A cause-and-effect relationship needs a plausible mechanism that explains how the input factor causes the outcome. Scientists would try to perform controlled experiments to show that other factors were not causing the carbon dioxide and air temperature to rise at the same time.

(c) A group of scientists perform an experiment which suggests that the rise in carbon dioxide levels does cause the increase in air temperature. Why is it important that their ideas are shared with other scientists? [1]

So that they can be peer reviewed.

(d) Many scientists say that governments should make new laws to reduce the carbon dioxide released from power stations and that money should be invested in renewable sources of energy. Suggest why governments might be reluctant to do this. [2]

It could increase the cost of electricity and reduce employment in power stations. The renewable energy sources might not be able to meet the energy demands of the population and there may be risks with the new technologies.

2. Iodine is an important chemical in our diets because it is an essential element in some hormones. In some countries, iodine compounds are added to table salt.

(a) To make iodine supplements to add to salt, Nick thinks he can extract iodine from seawater. He needs to find out how much iodine there is in seawater. Why should Nick test several samples of seawater, collected at different locations on different days? [1]

To ensure that the value from his experiment is a good measurement of the true value.

(b) The data that Nick collects are shown below. All measurements are in parts per million (ppm): 0.05; 0.04; 0.05; 0.05; 0.05; 0.06; 0.05; 0.01; 0.06. Which result is an outlier? [1]

0.01

Contents

Contents

B4 The Processes of Life

Cells

Cells are the building blocks of all living things.

All cells contain…
- **DNA**
- **organelles**.

DNA molecules are in the form of a **double helix** and contain the genetic code.

Organelles are the different parts of the cell's structure. They do different jobs within the cell and work together to allow the cell to perform a specific function.

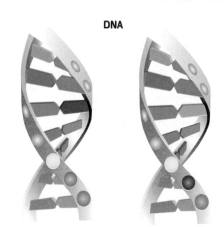

DNA

Animal Cells

Human cells, most animal cells and plant cells have the following parts:
- **Cytoplasm** – where most chemical reactions take place, including anaerobic respiration, the production of enzymes and other proteins.
- **Mitochondria** – contain the enzymes needed for aerobic respiration.
- A **nucleus** – contains the DNA that carries the genetic code for making enzymes and other proteins used in all chemical reactions in the cell.
- A **cell membrane** – allows chemicals like gases and water to pass in and out freely, but prevents other chemicals from leaving or entering the cell.

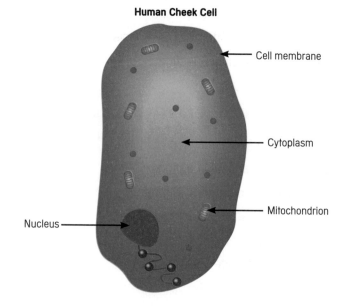

Human Cheek Cell

Cell membrane

Cytoplasm

Mitochondrion

Nucleus

Plant Cells

Plant cells also have the following parts:
- A **cell wall** – made of cellulose to strengthen the cell.
- A **permanent vacuole** – helps support the cell.
- **Chloroplasts** – contain the green pigment, chlorophyll (which absorbs light energy), and some enzymes needed for photosynthesis.

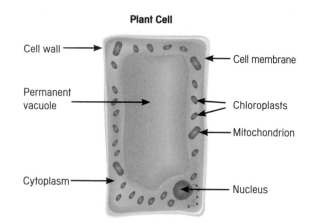

Plant Cell

Cell wall

Cell membrane

Permanent vacuole

Chloroplasts

Mitochondrion

Cytoplasm

Nucleus

Key Words   **DNA • Organelles • Nucleus**

Microbial Cells

Most microbial cells, e.g. bacteria, have the following features:

- **Cell wall** – **not** made of cellulose but of other material, e.g. protein.

- **DNA** – in a circular structure **not** in a nucleus and **not** as chromosomes.

Yeast cells are more similar to higher organisms, but are still referred to as microbial cells.

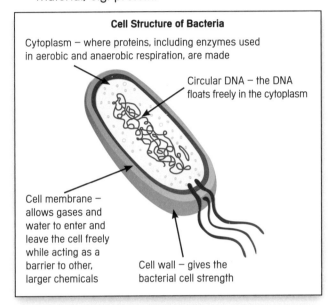

Cell Structure of Bacteria

Cytoplasm – where proteins, including enzymes used in aerobic and anaerobic respiration, are made

Circular DNA – the DNA floats freely in the cytoplasm

Cell membrane – allows gases and water to enter and leave the cell freely while acting as a barrier to other, larger chemicals

Cell wall – gives the bacterial cell strength

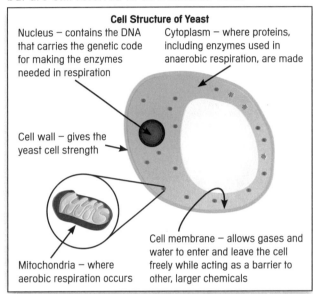

Cell Structure of Yeast

Nucleus – contains the DNA that carries the genetic code for making the enzymes needed in respiration

Cytoplasm – where proteins, including enzymes used in anaerobic respiration, are made

Cell wall – gives the yeast cell strength

Mitochondria – where aerobic respiration occurs

Cell membrane – allows gases and water to enter and leave the cell freely while acting as a barrier to other, larger chemicals

Enzymes

Enzymes are protein molecules that speed up the rate of chemical reactions in cells (i.e. they're catalysts in living things). Cells produce enzymes according to the instructions carried in genes (DNA code).

Enzymes need a specific temperature to work at their **optimum**. Different enzymes have different optimum working temperatures. The graph shows the effect of **temperature** on enzyme activity:

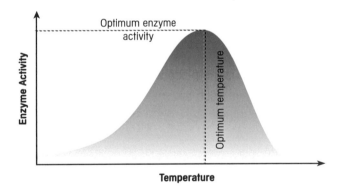

(HT) • At low temperatures, small increases in temperature cause an increase in the frequency and energy of collisions between reactants and enzymes, so the rate of reaction increases.

- After the **optimum enzyme activity** is reached, the enzymes start to get damaged, so the reaction starts to slow down.

- Eventually the enzyme's structure is permanently destroyed and it stops working.

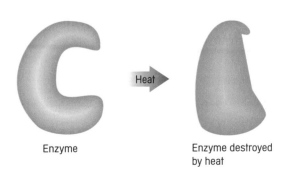

Enzyme

Heat

Enzyme destroyed by heat

(HT) In other words, the enzyme has become denatured.

B4 The Processes of Life

The Lock and Key Model

Only a molecule with the correct shape can fit into an enzyme. This is a bit like a **key** (the molecule) fitting into a **lock** (the enzyme). Once the enzyme and molecule are linked, the following happens:

1. The reaction takes place.
2. The products are released.
3. The process is able to start again.

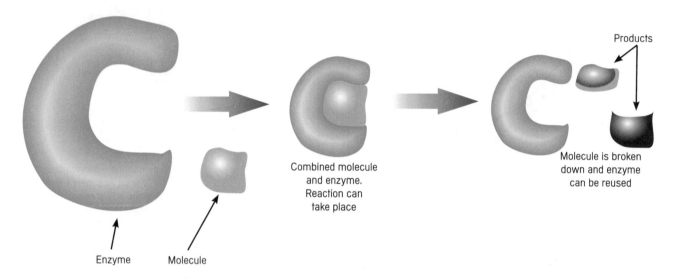

Enzyme   Molecule

Combined molecule and enzyme. Reaction can take place

Products

Molecule is broken down and enzyme can be reused

HT The Active Site

The **active site** is the place where the molecule fits into the enzyme. Each enzyme has a different **shape**, so it's highly specific.

The shape of the active site can be changed irreversibly by…
- **heating** the enzyme above a certain temperature
- altering the **pH level**.

This means the molecule can no longer fit and the reaction can't take place.

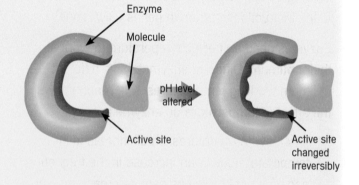

Enzyme

Molecule

pH level altered

Active site

Active site changed irreversibly

Respiration

Respiration is the **release of energy** from food chemicals in all living cells. There are two types of respiration:
- Aerobic respiration
- Anaerobic respiration.

Aerobic Respiration

Aerobic respiration releases energy inside living cells by breaking down glucose and combining the products with **oxygen**.

Glucose **+** Oxygen ⟶ Carbon dioxide **+** Water **+** Energy released

HT The **symbol** equation for this is:

$$C_6H_{12}O_6 + 6O_2 \longrightarrow 6CO_2 + 6H_2O + \text{Energy released}$$

Aerobic respiration needs oxygen and occurs in animal cells, plant cells and in many microbial cells. The energy released is used in many chemical reactions, including…

- movement, e.g. the contraction of muscles when running
- the synthesis (making) of large molecules from smaller ones, e.g. chlorophyll from glucose

HT • **active transport** of some chemical molecules across a cell membrane.

Anaerobic Respiration

Anaerobic respiration releases energy inside the cytoplasm of living cells by breaking down glucose molecules **without the use of oxygen**.

In plant cells and in some microbial cells, e.g. yeast:

Glucose ⟶ Carbon dioxide **+** Ethanol **+** Energy released

In animal cells and in some bacteria:

Glucose ⟶ Lactic acid **+** Energy released

Anaerobic respiration occurs in conditions of very low oxygen or where no oxygen is present. For example…

- when plant root cells are in waterlogged soil, e.g. rice plants
- in human muscle cells during vigorous exercise, e.g. a 100m sprint
- in bacterial cells inside a puncture wound.

Aerobic respiration is much more efficient and releases much more energy per glucose molecule (19 times more) than anaerobic respiration.

Quick Test

1. What is the function of mitochondria in a cell?
2. What are the three structures found in plant cells but not in animal cells?
3. What are enzymes?
4. What is respiration?
5. How is anaerobic respiration different from aerobic respiration?
6. HT What word describes an enzyme's structure when it's destroyed?

B4 The Processes of Life

Uses of Anaerobic Respiration

Anaerobic respiration can be useful:

- It provides a little more energy to cells when very necessary, e.g. to limb muscles when running away from danger.
- In sewage farms, anaerobic microbes can be added to the solid matter. These microbes break down the sewage and release methane gas, which is collected. This gas, now called **biogas**, is burned to heat water to turn a generator for electricity. Alternatively, biogas can be used as a fuel to replace petrol in vehicles.

- Anaerobic respiration in yeast is used in baking. Yeast in bread dough releases carbon dioxide gas, which makes the dough rise before baking.
- Anaerobic respiration in yeast is also used in brewing to produce alcohol (ethanol) in wines and beers. This process is known as **fermentation**. If oxygen gets in, the yeast stops respiring anaerobically and the alcohol turns to vinegar (ethanoic acid), which ruins the product.

Synthesis of Large Molecules

Glucose, produced in photosynthesis in plants, can be built up into a **polymer** as cellulose (for building cell walls) or as starch (for storage in roots).
A polymer is a long-chain molecule made from copies of the same unit – in this case, glucose.

Glucose		Starch
Individual sugar molecules	→	Long chains of identical sugar molecules

Glucose and nitrates can be joined to make larger molecules of amino acids. In turn, amino acids can be joined together to make proteins (**polymers** of amino acids) in plant, animal and bacterial cells.

Forming a Protein Molecule

Amino acids

Protein

Photosynthesis

Photosynthesis takes place in three stages:

1. **Light energy** is absorbed by **chlorophyll** in green plants.
2. Within the chlorophyll molecule, the light energy is used to **rearrange** the **atoms** of carbon dioxide and water to produce glucose (a sugar).
3. Oxygen is produced as a **waste product**.

The equation for photosynthesis is:

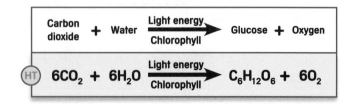

Carbon dioxide + Water $\xrightarrow[\text{Chlorophyll}]{\text{Light energy}}$ Glucose + Oxygen

HT $6CO_2 + 6H_2O \xrightarrow[\text{Chlorophyll}]{\text{Light energy}} C_6H_{12}O_6 + 6O_2$

Key Words   Polymer • Photosynthesis • Chlorophyll

Limiting Factors for Photosynthesis

Any one of the following factors can limit the rate of photosynthesis at a particular time:

- Temperature
- Carbon dioxide concentration
- Light intensity

Accurate measurements of the rate of photosynthesis can be hard because it's difficult to measure without altering one of the limiting factors. Factors that affect photosynthesis are difficult to control, e.g. wind or moisture levels.

Measurements only **indicate** the rate of photosynthesis rather than give a definite rate.

Temperature

1 As the temperature rises, so does the rate of photosynthesis. So, temperature is limiting the rate of photosynthesis.

2 As the temperature approaches 45°C, the enzymes controlling photosynthesis start to be destroyed and the rate of photosynthesis drops to zero.

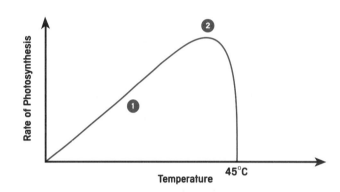

Carbon Dioxide Concentration

1 As the carbon dioxide concentration rises, so does the rate of photosynthesis. So, carbon dioxide is limiting the rate of photosynthesis.

2 A rise in carbon dioxide levels now has no effect. Carbon dioxide is no longer the limiting factor. It must be either light or temperature.

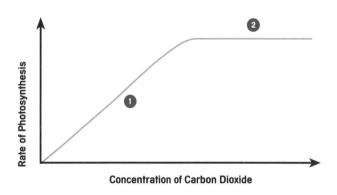

Light Intensity

1 As the light intensity increases, so does the rate of photosynthesis. So, light intensity is limiting the rate of photosynthesis.

2 A rise in light intensity now has no effect. Light intensity is no longer the limiting factor. It must be either carbon dioxide or temperature.

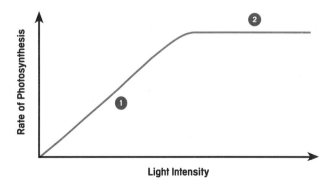

Collecting Data about how Light Affects Plants

Data can be collected in the field to investigate how light affects plants:

- Light levels can be measured using a **light meter**.
- Plants can be identified using an **identification key**.
- Plants are chosen at random by using a **quadrat** and **transect**.

A **quadrat** is anything with a defined area, e.g. a half metre square, which is placed at intervals along the transect line randomly to sample the area.

A **transect** is a random section across an area, e.g. a line or measured band, which is used to represent the entire area.

In the transect shown opposite, the quadrats are placed at 20-metre intervals, which would provide a good sample of the changes occurring along the transect line from the forest to the beach.

These techniques are used to ensure that the data produced is **representative** of the area but is also **random** to avoid any **bias** in the findings.

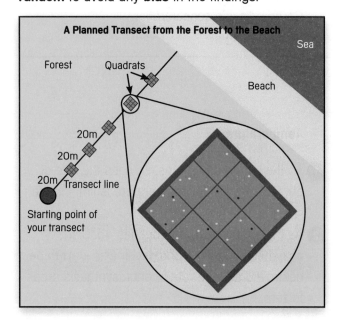

A Planned Transect from the Forest to the Beach

Sea

Forest   Quadrats

Beach

20m

20m

20m   Transect line

Starting point of your transect

Diffusion

Diffusion is the overall movement of **substances** from regions of **high** concentration, to regions of **low** concentration.

Oxygen and carbon dioxide are exchanged in the **leaf** by diffusion of the gases in and out.

Substances that move in and out of **cells** by diffusion include oxygen, carbon dioxide and dissolved food.

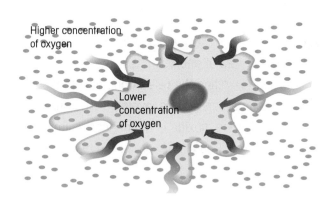

Higher concentration of oxygen

Lower concentration of oxygen

HT Energy Use in Plants

Plants need to absorb nitrates from the soil for healthy growth.

They normally absorb nutrients by **diffusion**, but the concentration of nitrates outside the plant is lower than that inside. Therefore, a plant has to use **energy** from respiration to absorb nitrates by **active transport**.

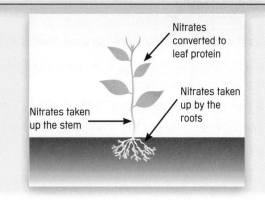

Nitrates converted to leaf protein

Nitrates taken up by the roots

Nitrates taken up the stem

HT Active Transport

Some chemicals can also be moved by active transport. This is the movement of a substance against a concentration gradient (i.e. from a region of low concentration to a region of high concentration). It requires **energy** from respiration to do this.

For example, if the concentration of glucose inside a cell is higher than the concentration outside the cell, the glucose would diffuse out of the cell along the concentration gradient. So, cells use active transport to bring all of the glucose back inside the cell.

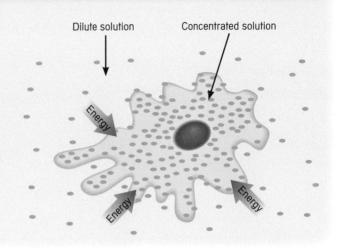

Osmosis

Osmosis is a type of diffusion. It's the overall movement of **water** from a **dilute solution** to a more **concentrated solution** through a partially permeable membrane.

The membrane allows the passage of water molecules but not solute molecules, which are too large.

The water moving due to osmosis gradually **dilutes** the concentrated solution.

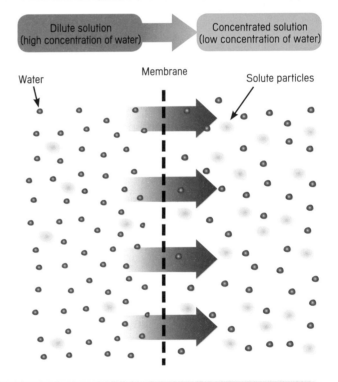

Quick Test

1. What is the green pigment that absorbs light energy in a plant cell?
2. What is the waste product of photosynthesis?
3. What do plants need from the soil to add to glucose to make amino acids?
4. What is a transect?
5. What is diffusion?
6. What is the only substance moved by osmosis?

1 **(a)** The diagram shows a human cheek cell.

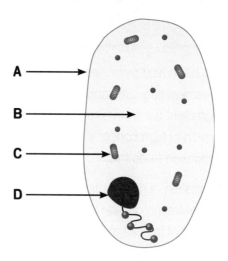

A ⟶

B ⟶

C ⟶

D ⟶

(i) Write the letter that identifies the part where aerobic respiration takes place. .... **[1]**

(ii) Write the letter that identifies the part which contains DNA. .... **[1]**

(b) What is the function of mitochondria? **[1]**

....

2 Cherry did an experiment to investigate the effect of light intensity on the rate of photosynthesis in a pondweed. In order to do this, she placed a light at different distances from the pondweed and collected the gas given off in a 10-minute period. Her results are shown on the right:

Distance from Light (cm)	Volume of Gas (cm³)
10	24
20	15
30	8
40	4

(a) What conclusion can Cherry make from these results? **[1]**

....

(b) What is the name of the gas given off by the pondweed? **[1]**

....

(c) Light intensity is a **limiting factor** on photosynthesis in this case. Name **one** other limiting factor on photosynthesis. **[1]**

....

3 Which of the following is the **incorrect** statement about aerobic respiration? Put a tick (✓) in the box next to the appropriate answer. **[1]**

Oxygen is used to break up glucose molecules. ☐

Ethanol is produced as a waste product. ☐

Energy is released and used in muscle contraction. ☐

Energy is released and used to build polymers in a cell. ☐

4 Hannah had two identical cylinders cut from the same potato. She placed one cylinder in a dish, labelled A, containing distilled water. She placed the other cylinder in a dish, labelled B, containing a strong sugar solution.

After 10 minutes she removed the potato cylinders. The cylinder from dish A had become very hard and stiff. The cylinder from dish B had become very soft and floppy.

(a) Why was it important to have the cylinders cut from the same potato? **[1]**

....

(b) What had caused the potato from dish A to go hard and stiff? **[1]**

....

(c) What had caused the potato from dish B to go soft and floppy? **[1]**

....

5 (a) Name **three** substances that are moved in and out of cells by diffusion. **[3]**

....

....

(b) Use the words provided to complete the following sentence about water movement into a cell. **[2]**

concentrated   partially   selectively   osmosis   diffusion   dilute   salt

When water moves across a .... permeable membrane from a

.... solution to a .... solution, it's called movement by

....

HT **6** This question is about enzymes.

(a) Some friends have just come out of a lesson about enzymes and are discussing it.

Sebastian
Enzymes are proteins.

Sarah
Enzymes work best at high temperatures.

Nicholas
Cells make enzymes according to instructions carried in the genes.

Adele
Enzymes are only involved in the breakdown of food in the gut.

Which two students give correct statements? **[2]**

.... and ....

(b) What is meant by the term **denatured**? **[1]**

....

B5 Growth and Development

The Development of Organisms

Living organisms are made up of cells. In multicellular organisms such as humans and plants...

- similar cells form a **tissue**
- groups of tissues form an **organ**
- groups of organs make up **systems** within the whole **organism**.

Cells divide by two processes:

- **Mitosis**
- **Meiosis**.

Cardiac muscle cell

Cardiac muscle tissue

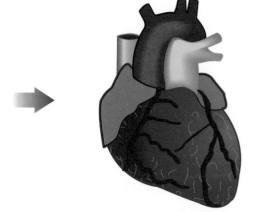
Heart (organ)

Mitosis

Mitosis is the division of body cells to produce new cells. Each new cell has...

- **identical** sets of **chromosomes** as the parent cell
- the **same number** of chromosomes as the parent cell
- the same genes as the parent cell.

Mitosis occurs...

- for growth
- for repair
- to replace old tissues.

To enable mitosis to take place, cells go through a cycle of **growth** and then **division**. The cycle repeats itself until the cell can no longer divide.

When a cell enters the **growth phase** of the cycle...

- the number of **organelles increase**
- the **chromosomes** are **copied** – the two strands of each DNA molecule separate and new strands form alongside them.

When a cell enters the **division phase** of the cycle...

- the copies of the **chromosomes separate**
- the cell **divides**.

Parent cell with two pairs of chromosomes.

Each chromosome copies itself.

The copies are pulled apart. Cell now divides for the only time in this mitosis sequence.

Two 'daughter' cells are formed.

Tissue • Organ • Mitosis • Meiosis • Chromosome

Meiosis

Meiosis only takes place in the **testes** and **ovaries** and is a special type of cell division that produces **gametes** (sex cells, e.g. egg and sperm) for sexual reproduction.

Gametes contain **half** the number of chromosomes as the parent cell.

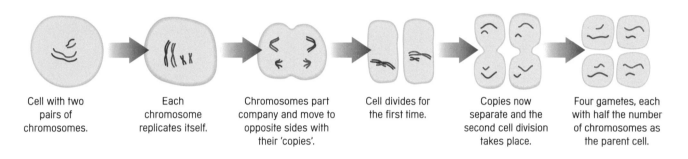

| Cell with two pairs of chromosomes. | Each chromosome replicates itself. | Chromosomes part company and move to opposite sides with their 'copies'. | Cell divides for the first time. | Copies now separate and the second cell division takes place. | Four gametes, each with half the number of chromosomes as the parent cell. |

Fertilisation

During **fertilisation** a **male gamete** (sperm) and a **female gamete** (egg) fuse together to produce a single body cell, called a **zygote**.

Gametes only have half the number of **chromosomes** as the parent cell, so the zygote that's produced has **one whole set** of chromosomes.

In each new pair of chromosomes…
- one chromosome comes from the father
- one chromosome comes from the mother.

The zygote then divides by **mitosis** to produce a cluster of cells called an **embryo**.

The embryo continues to divide by mitosis (from one cell to two, to four, to eight, etc.), after which the cells become specialised, until birth as a fully developed baby.

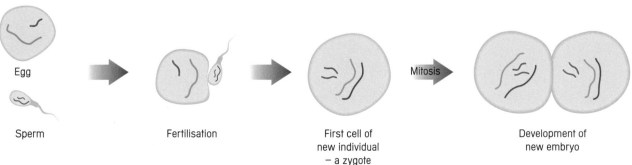

| Egg / Sperm | Fertilisation | First cell of new individual – a zygote | Mitosis | Development of new embryo |

B5 Growth and Development

Variation

Meiosis and **sexual reproduction** produce **variation** between offspring and parents:

- When the gametes fuse, genetic information from two individuals is combined.
- For each gene, just one of each parent's alleles is passed on.
- Each offspring can have a different combination of alleles from either parent.
- The offspring have different characteristics from each other.

Genes

Genes are present in the **chromosomes** in each cell **nucleus**.

Genes control…
- growth and development in organisms
- the development of characteristics, e.g. eye colour.

Genetic Code

Genes control **characteristics** by providing instructions for the production of **proteins**.

The instructions are in the form of a **code**, made up of **four bases** that hold the two strands of the double helix of the **DNA molecule** together. These bases always pair up in the same way:
- Adenine (A) pairs with thymine (T).
- Cytosine (C) pairs with guanine (G).

A gene is a small section of DNA within the chromosome. The order of the bases in the DNA section is the genetic code for the production of a particular protein. This is how the code determines the end characteristics of any organism.

A Section of DNA

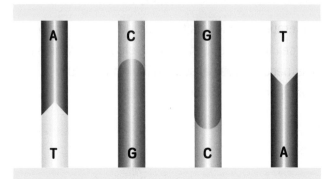

Controlling Growth and Development

DNA is **too large** to leave the nucleus. The genes therefore stay inside the nucleus but the production of proteins takes place **outside** the nucleus, in the **cytoplasm**.

Information stored in the genes has to be transferred into the cytoplasm.

This transfer is done in the following way:
1. The relevant section of DNA is unzipped.
2. Instructions are copied onto smaller molecules.

HT The smaller molecules are called **messenger RNA (mRNA)**.

3. These molecules leave the nucleus and carry the instructions to the **ribosomes**.
4. The ribosomes follow the instructions to make the relevant protein.

HT The sequence of bases in a gene determines the order in which **amino acids** are joined together to make a particular **protein**.

A group of **three** base pairs codes for one amino acid in a protein chain, called a **triplet code**. There are 20 different amino acids that can be made.

The structure of the protein depends on the amino acids that make it up.

This process is as follows:
1. DNA unravels at the correct gene.
2. A copy of the coding strand is made to produce mRNA.
3. The mRNA copy moves from the nucleus into the cytoplasm.
4. The triplet code is decoded by the ribosomes.
5. Amino acids are joined together to form a polypeptide (protein).

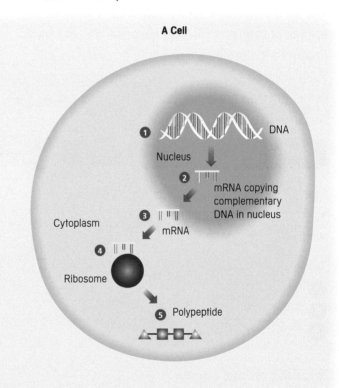

A Cell

DNA

Nucleus

mRNA copying complementary DNA in nucleus

Cytoplasm

mRNA

Ribosome

Polypeptide

Quick Test

1. What is a tissue?
2. Name the process by which body cells divide to produce new identical cells.
3. Where are gametes produced in the human body?
4. What is the name of the single cell produced after the fertilisation of an egg cell by a sperm cell?
5. What is the missing word? Adenine, cytosine, thymine and guanine are the four .... in a DNA molecule.
6. HT What carries the genetic information from the DNA in the nucleus to the cytoplasm?

Key Words   Messenger RNA (mRNA)

B5 Growth and Development

Development of New Organisms

Up to the 8 cell stage, all cells in a human **embryo**...
- are unspecialised
- can have any gene switched on to form **any** kind of specialised cell.

These cells are known as **embryonic stem cells**.

After the 8 cell stage, the cells in an embryo...
- become **specialised**
- form different types of **tissue**.

The cells contain the **same genes**, but many genes are **not active** (switched off) because the cell only produces the **proteins** it needs to carry out its role. In specialised cells, only the genes needed for the cell to function are active (switched on) as it only requires specific proteins (mainly enzymes).

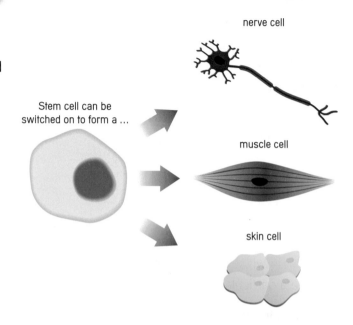

Stem cell can be switched on to form a ...

nerve cell

muscle cell

skin cell

Stem Cells

Stem cells could potentially be used to...
- help treat diseases and disorders
- repair damage to various tissues.

There are three sources of stem cells:
1. Embryos
2. Blood from the umbilical cord
3. Adult stem cells from bone marrow.

Only the **embryonic stem cells** are completely unspecialised and can be used to form any cell type.

Ethical decisions need to be taken when using embryonic stem cells and this work is subject to government regulation.

(HT) In **therapeutic cloning**...
- the nucleus is removed from an egg cell and replaced with a nucleus from one of the patient's cells
- the egg cell is then stimulated so that it starts to divide (as if it were a zygote)
- at the 8 cell stage, cells can be removed as they're still unspecialised.

Adult stem cells will only produce cells of a certain type. For example, cells for creating blood cells in bone marrow have to be encouraged to grow more of that type of cell by reactivating (switching back on) inactive genes in the nuclei.

The advantage of using adult cells for growing replacement tissue is that they can be taken from the patient, so the patient's immune system will not reject the transplant.

Replacement tissue can be grown in a laboratory. Sometimes a 'host animal' (e.g. a mouse) is used to maintain a blood supply during growth.

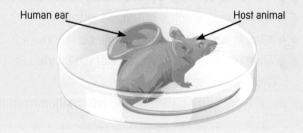

Human ear   Host animal

Differentiation in Plants

Plant cells divide by the process of **mitosis**.

New cells in plants specialise into the cells of…
- roots
- leaves
- flowers.

Unlike animals, most plants continue to grow in **height** and **width** throughout their lives.

Flowers

Leaves

Root

Meristems

Plant growth only occurs in areas called **meristems**, which are sites where **unspecialised cells** are dividing by **mitosis**.

These cells then…
- differentiate
- become specialised.

There are **two types** of meristem:
- **Lateral**, which leads to increased girth.
- **Apical**, which leads to increased height and longer roots.

Some plant cells remain **unspecialised** and can develop into any type of plant cell. These cells allow **clones** of plants with desirable features to be produced from **cuttings**.

If the **hormonal conditions** in their environment are changed, the unspecialised plant cells can develop into other…
- **tissues**, e.g. xylem and phloem
- **organs**, e.g. leaves, roots and flowers.

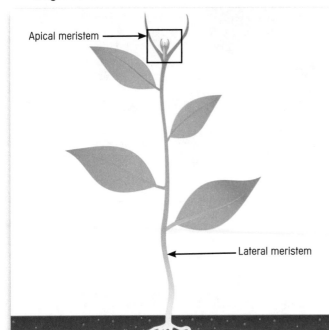

Apical meristem

Lateral meristem

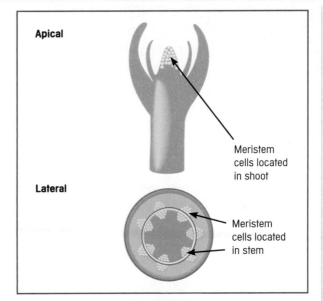

Apical

Lateral

Meristem cells located in shoot

Meristem cells located in stem

B5 Growth and Development

Xylem and Phloem

Xylem tubes are used by the plant to…

- transport water and soluble mineral salts from the roots to the stem and leaves
- replace water lost during transpiration and photosynthesis.

Phloem tubes are used by the plant to transport dissolved food to the whole plant for respiration or storage.

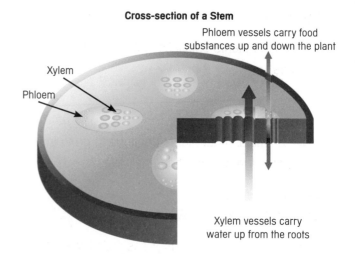

Cross-section of a Stem

Phloem vessels carry food substances up and down the plant

Xylem

Phloem

Xylem vessels carry water up from the roots

Cuttings

Plants can be reproduced in the following way:

1 Cuttings are taken from a plant.
2 The cuttings are put in a rooting hormone.
3 Roots start to form and the new plants develop.

The new plants are **genetically identical** to the parent plant, i.e. they are **clones**.

(HT) **Auxins** are the main plant hormones used in horticulture, which…

- affect cell division at the tip of a shoot
- cause cells to grow in size just under the tip so that the stem or roots grow longer.

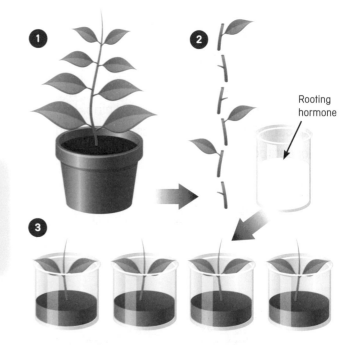

1

2

Rooting hormone

3

Phototropism

Plants respond to light by changing the direction in which they grow. This is called **phototropism**.

They grow towards a light source as they need light to survive.

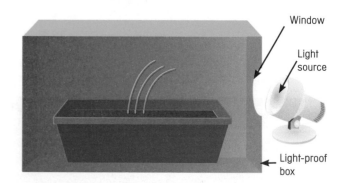

Window

Light source

Light-proof box

Key Words   **Clone • Auxin • Phototropism**

HT How Phototropism Works

Auxin is produced at the shoot tip. It moves down the shoot, causing cells further down the shoot to grow.

When light shines on a shoot, auxin near the light source is slowly destroyed, so there's more auxin on the far side away from the light. This causes these cells to lengthen faster than those near the light, so the shoot bends towards the light. Experiments, like the ones below, have allowed scientists to achieve this explanation of phototropism.

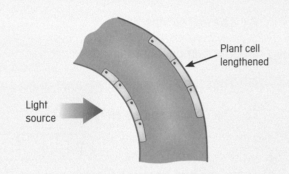

Plant cell lengthened

Light source

1 When a light source is directly overhead...
- auxin is evenly spread through the shoot
- the shoot grows **straight** up.

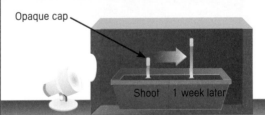

2 When a light source is at an angle...
- auxin is destroyed nearest to the light source
- the auxin is concentrated on the side furthest away from the light
- the shoot **bends** towards the light.

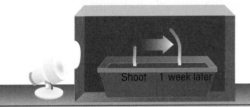

3 If the tip of the shoot is removed or covered in opaque material, then the plant will continue to grow upwards – as if the light source isn't there.

Opaque cap

Shoot   1 week later

4 If the tip is covered with a transparent cap, then it will still grow towards the light source. The same thing will happen if an opaque cylinder is wrapped around the stem, leaving the tip exposed.

Transparent cap   Opaque cylinder

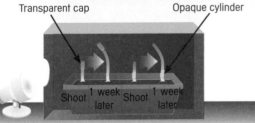

Shoot 1 week later Shoot 1 week later

Quick Test

1 What is the name given to the areas of plants where growth occurs?
2 Which tubes carry water up a plant?
3 Which tubes carry dissolved food in a plant?
4 What is needed for a cutting from a plant to develop roots?
5 Plants grow towards light. What is this called?

1 **(a)** These steps describe cell growth and division in the cell cycle. They're in the wrong order. Put the steps in the correct order by writing letters in the empty boxes. One has been done for you. **[2]**

  A The cell divides.

  B The number of organelles increases.

  C The chromosome copies move apart from one another.

  D The chromosomes are copied.

  [B | | |]

(b) Name the **two** locations that the process of meiosis can take place in. **[2]**

....

....

(c) What is the name given to a fertilised cell? **[1]**

....

2 Jonah planted a seedling (a young plant) into a flowerpot and placed it in a greenhouse. His sister moved it so that the Sun only shone on it from one side.

Explain how the seedling would grow and why this would help it to survive. **[6]**

  🖉 *The quality of written communication will be assessed in your answer to this question.*

....

....

....

....

....

....

....

3 **(a)** What are the characteristics of stem cells? **[1]**

....

(b) Why can't stem cells be taken after the 8 cell stage? **[1]**

....

(c) Why are embryonic stem cells sometimes better to use than adult stem cells? **[1]**

....

....

4 Jonty was investigating the growth rate of different bacteria over a three-hour period. He began with a single bacterium and his table of results is below.

Type	30 minutes	60 minutes	90 minutes	120 minutes	150 minutes	180 minutes
A	2	8	12	16	32	64
B	4	16	64	256	1024	4096
C	2	8	16	16	32	64
D	4	16	32	128	256	1024

(a) Describe **two** differences between the pattern of results shown by type B and type D bacteria over the period of investigation. **[2]**

....

....

(b) Jonty concluded that the highest rate of cell division was between 30 and 60 minutes. Suggest one source of evidence in the table that doesn't support his conclusion. **[1]**

....

....

HT **5** **(a)** After a revision lesson about genes and DNA, five pupils discuss some of the main points.

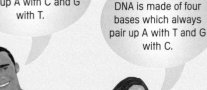
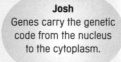

Mark
The human DNA molecule is a circular shape.

Chloe
I think the DNA molecule has a double helix structure.

Imran
DNA is made of four bases which always pair up A with C and G with T.

Emily
DNA is made of four bases which always pair up A with T and G with C.

Josh
Genes carry the genetic code from the nucleus to the cytoplasm.

Which two pupils are giving correct statements? **[2]**

.... and ....

(b) DNA is too large to leave the cell. How does the genetic information leave the cell? **[1]**

....

B6 Brain and Mind

The Central Nervous System

A **stimulus** is a change in an organism's environment. Animals respond to **stimuli** in order to keep themselves in suitable conditions for survival.

An animal's response is coordinated by the **central nervous system** (**CNS**). This part of the system is sometimes referred to as the **processing centre**. The CNS (brain and spinal cord) is connected to the body by the **peripheral nervous system** (**PNS**).

The peripheral nervous system consists of…
- **sensory neurons** that carry impulses from **receptors** to the CNS
- **motor neurons** that carry impulses from the CNS to **effectors**.

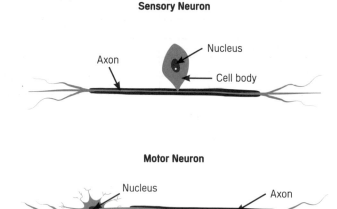

Sensory Neuron

Axon · Nucleus · Cell body

Motor Neuron

Nucleus · Axon · Cell body

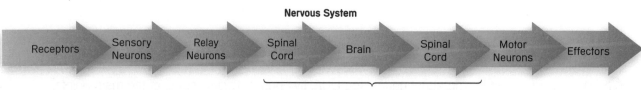

Nervous System

Receptors → Sensory Neurons → Relay Neurons → Spinal Cord → Brain → Spinal Cord → Motor Neurons → Effectors

The Central Nervous System (CNS)

Receptors and Effectors

Receptors and **effectors** can form part of complex organs, for example…
- muscle cells in a muscle
- light receptor cells in the retina of the eye
- hormone secreting cells in a gland.

Muscle cells in a muscle – impulses travel along motor neurons and stop at the muscle cells (effectors), causing the muscle cells to contract.

Light receptor cells in the retina of the eye – the lens focuses light onto receptor cells in the retina. The receptor cells are then stimulated and send impulses along sensory neurons to the brain.

Hormone secreting cells in a gland – an impulse travels along a motor neuron and stops at the hormone secreting cells in glands (effectors). This triggers the release of the hormone into the bloodstream.

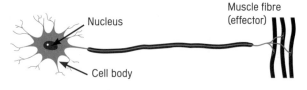

A Motor Neuron

Nucleus · Muscle fibre (effector) · Cell body

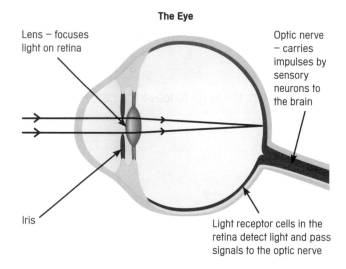

The Eye

Lens – focuses light on retina

Optic nerve – carries impulses by sensory neurons to the brain

Iris

Light receptor cells in the retina detect light and pass signals to the optic nerve

Key Words   Stimulus • Central nervous system • Neuron • Receptor • Effector

Neurons

Neurons are specially-adapted cells that carry an **electrical signal** when stimulated:

- They are **elongated** (lengthened) to make connections between different parts of your body.
- They have **branched endings** so that a single neuron can act on many other neurons or effectors.

In **motor neurons** the cytoplasm forms a long fibre surrounded by a cell membrane called an **axon**.

Some axons are surrounded by a fatty sheath, which…

- insulates the neuron from neighbouring cells
- increases the speed at which the nerve impulse is transmitted.

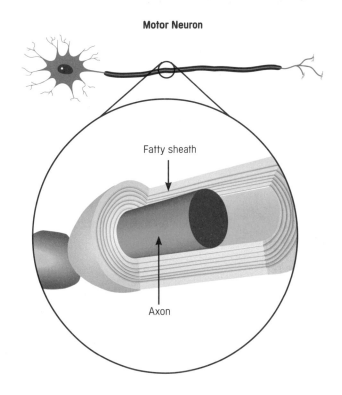

Motor Neuron

Fatty sheath

Axon

Synapses

Synapses are the gaps between adjacent neurons.

(HT) Impulses are transferred between neurons in the following way:

1. A nerve impulse reaches the synapse through the sensory neuron.
2. The impulse triggers the release of chemicals, called neurotransmitters, into the synapse.
3. Neurotransmitters diffuse across the synapse and bind with receptor molecules on the membrane of a motor neuron.
4. A nerve impulse is sent through the motor neuron.

The receptor molecules only bind with certain chemicals to start a nerve impulse in the motor neuron.

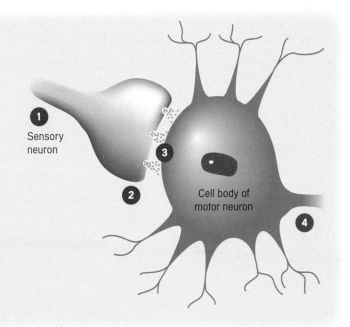

1 Sensory neuron

2

3

Cell body of motor neuron

4

Reflex Actions

A **reflex action** is a fast, automatic, involuntary response to a **stimulus**.

The basic pathway for a reflex arc is as follows:

1. A **receptor** is stimulated (e.g. by a sharp pain).
2. This causes impulses to pass along a **sensory neuron** into the spinal cord.
3. The sensory neuron **synapses** with a relay neuron, by-passing the brain.
4. The relay neuron synapses with a motor neuron, sending impulses to the **effectors**.
5. The effectors **respond** (e.g. muscles contract).

Simple reflexes like these ensure that an animal **automatically responds** to a **stimulus** in a way that helps it to survive, for example...

- finding food
- sheltering from predators
- finding a mate.

HT The fixed pathway of neurons in these actions allows the very rapid response as there isn't any processing of the information by the brain.

The majority of the behaviour displayed by simple animals is the result of **reflex actions**. The disadvantage of this is that the animals have difficulty responding to new situations.

Reflex Action Pathway

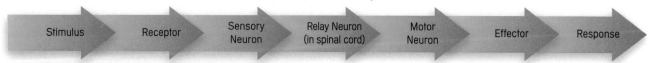

| Stimulus | Receptor | Sensory Neuron | Relay Neuron (in spinal cord) | Motor Neuron | Effector | Response |

Simple Reflexes in Humans

Newborn babies exhibit a range of simple reflexes:

- **Stepping reflex** – when held under its arms in an upright position, with feet on a firm surface, a baby makes walking movements with its legs.
- **Grasping reflex** – baby tightly grasps a finger that is placed in its hand.
- **Rooting reflex** – baby turns head and opens mouth ready to feed when its cheek is stroked.
- **Sucking reflex** – baby sucks on a finger (or mother's nipple) that is put in its mouth.

Adults also display a range of simple reflexes. For example, the **pupil reflex** in your eye stops bright light from damaging your retina. Your iris controls the amount of light that enters your eye by contracting various muscle fibres.

Other reflexes include...

- the 'knee-jerk' when the leg straightens if the knee joint is struck beneath the knee cap
- dropping a hot object when you grip it
- blinking when an object comes close to your face.

Eye in Dim Light

Increased pupil size

Radial muscles contract

Circular muscles relax

Eye in Bright Light

Decreased pupil size

Radial muscles relax

Circular muscles contract

The Pupil Reflex

| Light on retina | Impulse via optic nerve to the brain | Impulse via motor nerve to iris muscles | Pupil changes size |

Conditioned Reflexes

A reflex response to a new stimulus can be learned by building an association between the stimulus that naturally triggers the response (**primary stimulus**) and the new stimulus (**secondary stimulus**).

The resulting reflex is called a **conditioned reflex action**.

This effect was discovered at the beginning of the 20th century by a Russian scientist named Pavlov.

Pavlov carried out the following dog experiment:
1. A bell was rung repeatedly whenever meat was shown and given to the dog.
2. Eventually, ringing the bell without any meat present caused the dog to salivate.

A further example might be the feeling of hunger you get just by looking at the time on the clock. You've been conditioned to feel hungry at that time, even if you're not actually hungry.

(HT) In a conditioned reflex, the final response has **no direct connection** to the stimulus.

Some conditioned reflexes can increase a species' chance of survival.

For example, the caterpillar of the cinnabar moth is black and orange in colour, to warn predators that it's poisonous. After eating a few cinnabar caterpillars, a bird will start to associate these colours with a very unpleasant taste and avoid eating anything that is black and orange in colour.

In this way, a conditioned reflex may be regarded as simple learning.

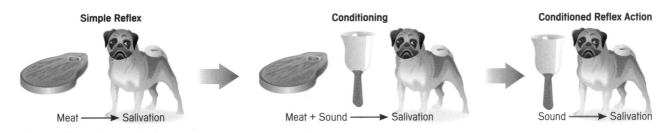

| Simple Reflex | Conditioning | Conditioned Reflex Action |
| Meat → Salivation | Meat + Sound → Salivation | Sound → Salivation |

(HT) Modifying Reflex Actions

In some situations your brain can override or modify a reflex action by sending a signal, via a neuron, to the motor neuron in the reflex arc.

For example, this modification allows you to keep hold of a hot plate even though your body's natural reflex response is to drop it.

Quick Test

1. What is a stimulus?
2. What type of neuron carries impulses from the central nervous system to an effector such as a muscle?
3. What is the name of a gap between two neurons?
4. What is the name of the long fibre attached to the cell body in a motor neuron?
5. What is a reflex action?
6. What is the name given to the type of action when the final response has no direct connection to the stimulus?

B6 Brain and Mind

Neuron Pathways

Mammals have **complex brains** that contain billions of **neurons**. This allows them to learn from experience, including how to respond to different situations (**social behaviour**).

In mammals **neuron pathways** are formed in the brain during development.

The brain grows rapidly during the first few years after birth. As each neuron matures, it sends out multiple branches, increasing the number of **synapses**.

The way in which a mammal interacts with its environment determines which pathways are formed:

1. Each time you have a new experience, a different neuron pathway is stimulated.
2. Every time the experience is repeated after that, the pathway is strengthened.
3. Pathways that aren't used regularly are eventually deleted.
4. Only the pathways that are activated most frequently are preserved.

These modifications mean that certain pathways of your brain become more likely to transmit impulses than others and you will learn how to do a task.

This is why you're able to learn some skills through **repetition**, for example, riding a bicycle, revising for an exam or playing a musical instrument.

A **PET** (Positron Emission Tomography) **scan** provides a 3D image, which shows neuron activity in parts of the brain in response to learning words through…
- hearing them
- seeing them
- speaking them.

The areas that are stimulated the most develop more synapses between neurons.

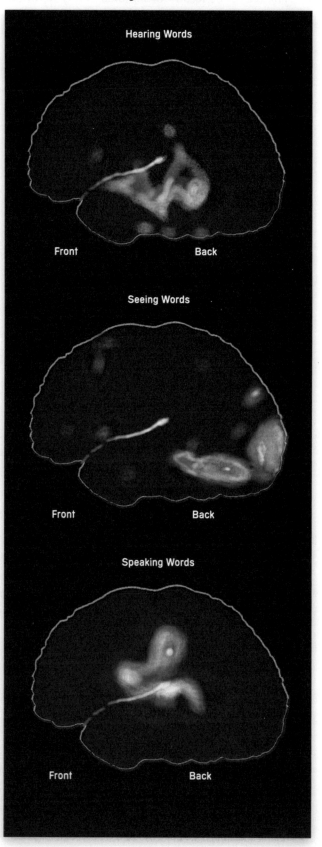

Image of a PET Scan

Hearing Words

Front   Back

Seeing Words

Front   Back

Speaking Words

Front   Back

HT Children

Child Development

After children are born, there are a series of developmental milestones that can be checked to see if development is following normal patterns.

If the milestones are missing or late it could mean that…
- there are neurological problems
- the child is lacking stimulation.

For example…
- at three months, babies should be able to lift their heads when held to someone's shoulder
- at 12 months, babies should be able to hold a cup and drink from it.

Feral Children

Evidence suggests that children only learn some skills at particular stages in their development.

One example of evidence showing this comes from the study of language development in 'feral children'.

Feral children have been isolated from society in some way, so they don't go through the normal development process.

This isolation can be deliberate (e.g. keeping a child alone in a locked room) or accidental (e.g. through being shipwrecked).

In the absence of any other humans, the children don't ever gain the ability to talk, other than to make rudimentary grunting noises.

Learning a language later in development is a much harder and slower process.

Adapting

The variety of potential pathways in the brain makes it possible for animals to **adapt** to new situations.

For example…
- dogs can be trained to follow spoken commands
- dolphins in captivity can be trained to collect food from a person's hand.

Coordination of Senses

The evolution of a large brain, containing billions of neurons, gave humans a better chance of survival due to the ability to arrive at complex conclusions quickly in different situations.

Intelligence, memory, language and consciousness (a sense of right and wrong) are some of the skills that enable human survival. These are all dealt with in the **cerebral cortex** area of the brain.

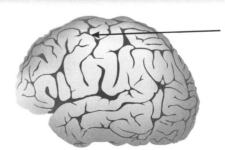

Cerebral cortex

Key Words | Cerebral cortex | 29

B6 Brain and Mind

Mapping the Cortex

Scientists have used different methods to map the regions of the cerebral cortex:
- Physiological techniques
- Electronic techniques
- Magnetic Resonance Images (MRI) scanning.

Physiological techniques – damage to different parts of the brain can produce different problems, e.g. memory loss, paralysis or speech loss. Studying the effects of this has led to an understanding of which parts of the brain control different functions.

Electronic techniques – an electroencephalogram (EEG) is a visual record of the electrical activity generated by **neurons** in the brain. Electrodes are placed on the scalp to pick up the electrical signals. By stimulating the patient's **receptors**, the parts of the brain that respond can be mapped.

Magnetic Resonance Imaging (MRI) scanning
– this is a relatively new technique that can be used to produce images of different cross-sections of the brain. The computer-generated picture uses colour to represent different levels of electrical activity. The activity in the brain changes depending on what the person is doing or thinking.

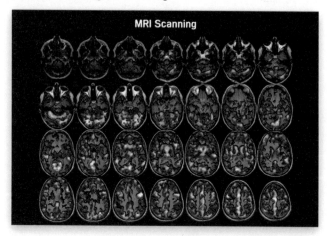

MRI Scanning

Memory

Memory is the ability to **store** and **retrieve** information. It can be divided into…
- **short-term memory** – stores information for a limited period of time
- **long-term memory** – stores an unlimited amount of information.

Many scientists have produced **models** to try to explain how the brain stores information, e.g. the **multi-store model**. This model states that short-term memory can be rehearsed so that it enters long-term storage.

Like many models though, this doesn't fully explain memory, as it's been found that information **doesn't** need short-term rehearsal to be stored as long-term memory. So, scientists may disagree about the explanations but continue their research to try to support or reject hypotheses to achieve a better conclusion.

Why we **forget** isn't fully explained by the model either. The reasons may be…
- **physical** – neurons decaying, e.g. in Alzheimer's disease
- **lack of retrieval** – if we don't use the information for a long time, the pathway is lost.

You're more likely to remember information if…
- it's repeated (especially over an extended period of time)
- there's a strong **stimulus** associated with it, e.g. colour, light, smell or sound
- you can see a pattern in it or impose a pattern on it, e.g. the order of the planets can be remembered by imposing a pattern: **M**r **V**enus's **e**lephant **m**akes **j**am **s**itting **u**pon **n**ectarines – **M**ercury, **V**enus, **E**arth, **M**ars, **J**upiter, **S**aturn, **U**ranus and **N**eptune.

Drugs and the Nervous System

Some drugs and toxins, e.g. Ecstasy, beta blockers and Prozac, affect the nervous system by changing the speed at which nerve impulses travel to the brain.

They can also…
- send false signals to the brain
- prevent nerve impulses from travelling across **synapses**
- overload the nervous system with too many nerve impulses.

HT **Serotonin** is a chemical transmitter used in the **central nervous system**. It can have mood-enhancing effects, i.e. it's associated with feeling happy.

Serotonin passes across the brain's synapses, landing on receptor molecules. Serotonin not on a receptor is absorbed back into the transmitting neuron by the transporter molecules.

Ecstasy (MDMA) blocks the transporter sites causing serotonin to build up in the synapse. This causes…
- serotonin concentrations in the brain to increase
- the user to experience feelings of elation.

The neurons are harmed in this process and memory loss can be caused in the long term.

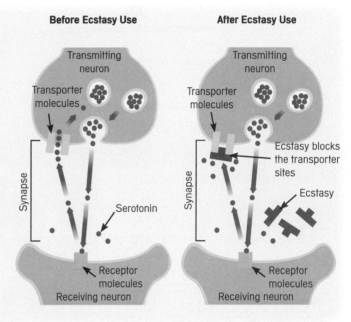

Coordination in the Body

All nervous responses can bring about fast responses, but they don't last long – they're immediate and short-lived.

Hormones produced in glands (e.g. insulin, adrenalin and oestrogen) travel in the blood and so can move all around the body. The response can last a lot longer in this way but is slower to act.

Both of these systems, nervous and chemical, are necessary to control the body's functions and have evolved in many multicellular organisms.

Quick Test

1. What develop in the human brain to allow learning from experience, e.g. language?
2. Which part of the brain is most concerned with intelligence and memory?
3. Name the technique that produces images of cross-sections of the brain.
4. What is memory?
5. What is the 'type' of memory when the brain only stores information for a limited time?
6. How do drugs like Ecstasy and Prozac affect the nervous system?

B6 Exam Practice Questions

1 (a) Put a (ring) around the correct choice to complete each sentence.

(i) Animals respond to stimuli. These responses are coordinated by the **central nervous system / peripheral nervous system**. **[1]**

(ii) The system making up the connections of sensory and motor neurons is called the **central nervous system / peripheral nervous system**. **[1]**

(b) What type of neurons do the diagrams below show?

(i) **[1]**

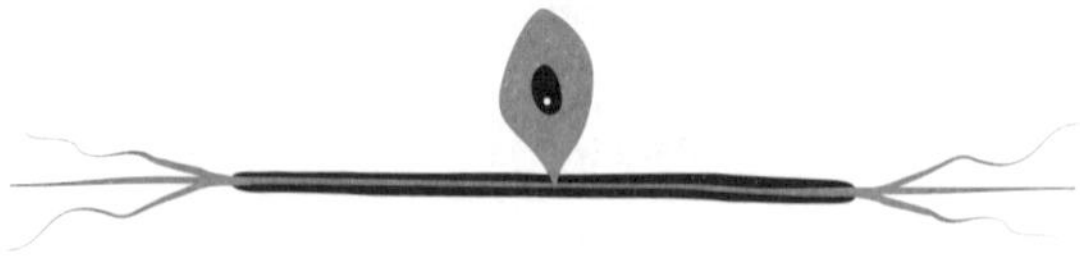

....

(ii) **[1]**

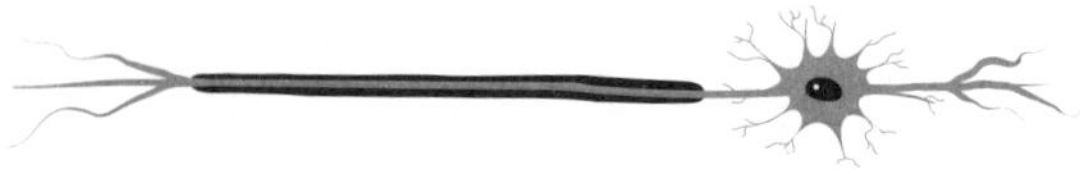

....

(c) What does a motor neuron do to a hormone secreting gland when a message is sent? **[1]**

....

(d) Give **two** functions of the fatty sheath surrounding the axon. **[2]**

....

....

(e) What are synapses? **[1]**

....

(f) How do drugs in general affect the nervous system? **[1]**

....

2 Raul picks up a plate with his dinner on it and immediately drops it because it's far too hot. This is an example of a reflex action. Explain as fully as you can the sequence of events that take place in Raul's nervous system for this to happen. **[6]**

✎ *The quality of written communication will be assessed in your answer to this question.*

....

....

....

....

....

....

3 The following table shows the reaction times of a patient who has been given varying doses of a drug.

Drug Dose	Time Taken to React (seconds)		
	Experiment 1	Experiment 2	Experiment 3
Nil	1.02	1.04	1.02
Small	1.32	1.08	1.04
Medium	1.18	1.19	1.24
Large	2.30	2.40	2.42

(a) Which of the reaction times appears to be an outlier? [1]

....

(b) What conclusion can you suggest from the data? [1]

....

(c) Why was each reaction time repeated three times? [1]

....

4 What is needed before biologists will accept a new theory on memory?
Put ticks (✓) in the boxes next to the **three** correct answers. [2]

The theory must…

…have a scientific mechanism. ☐   …be easy to understand. ☐

…be from a qualified biologist. ☐   …be published. ☐

…have data with high variability. ☐   …be repeatable. ☐

HT **5** (a) These steps describe the sequence of nerve impulse transmission. They're in the wrong order.
Put the steps into the correct order by writing the letters in the empty boxes. One has been done for you. [3]

   A   Nerve impulse is sent through motor neuron.

   B   Chemical neurotransmitters are released into synapse.

   C   Neurotransmitters bind with receptors on motor neuron.

   D   Nerve impulse moves through sensory neuron.

   E   Neurotransmitters diffuse across.

   | D | | | |

(b) Which drug blocks the sites in the brain's synapses where serotonin is removed? [1]

....

C4 Chemical Patterns

The Periodic Table

An **element** is made of only one kind of **atom**. All the atoms of an element have the same number of **protons**.

Different **elements** have different **proton numbers** and they're arranged in order of increasing proton number in the **modern periodic table**. This gives repeating **patterns** in the **properties** of elements.

You can use the periodic table as a reference table to obtain the following information about the elements:
- Relative atomic mass – the total number of protons and **neutrons** in an atom
- Symbol
- Name
- Atomic (proton) number – the number of protons (and also the number of **electrons**) in an atom.

You can also tell if elements are **metals** or **non-metals** by looking at their position in the table.

N.B. You will be given a copy of the periodic table in the exam. You can find one at the back of this book.

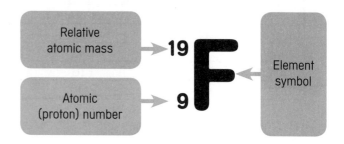

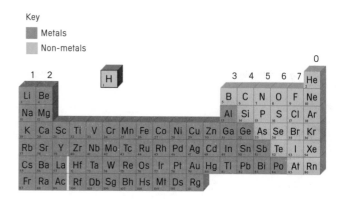

Groups

A **vertical column** of elements is called a **group**. Elements that are in the same group have **similar properties**.

Group 1 elements include…
- lithium (Li)
- sodium (Na)
- potassium (K).

The group number corresponds to the number of electrons in the outer shell of an atom. For example…
- **Group 1** elements have **one electron** in their outer shell
- **Group 7** elements have **seven electrons** in their outer shell.

Periods

A **horizontal row** of elements is called a **period**. Examples of elements in the same period are lithium (Li), carbon (C) and neon (Ne).

The period number corresponds to how many shells there are in an atom of a particular element. For example, elements with three shells are found in the third period.

The Development of the Periodic Table

Many years ago, scientists identified elements as chemicals that couldn't be broken down. Some scientists tried to find patterns in these elements, but other scientists didn't think that this would be possible.

In 1817, **Döbereiner** realised that some elements with similar properties formed groups of three. He called these **triads**. One example is lithium, sodium and potassium. Another is chlorine, bromine and iodine.

In 1865, **Newlands** suggested that when the elements were arranged in order of increasing atomic weight, some repeating patterns in properties could be seen. He called this the **law of octaves**, after the musical scale. Other scientists thought this was ridiculous.

In 1869, **Mendeleev** presented his periodic table, which is much like the one we use today. His table allowed **similar elements to be grouped together** and also showed the **repeating patterns** that other chemists had noticed.

Mendeleev deliberately left some gaps in his periodic table, which were for elements that he suggested hadn't been discovered yet. He even correctly predicted the properties of these elements.

New technologies have been very important in discovering new elements. For example, **spectroscopy** helped to discover the noble gases, which Mendeleev didn't include in his periodic table because none of them had yet been found.

Atoms

An **atom** has a **small central nucleus**, made up of **protons** and **neutrons**. The nucleus is surrounded by **electrons,** which are arranged in **shells** (**energy levels**).

An atom has the same number of protons as electrons, so the atom as a whole is **neutral** (i.e. it has no electrical charge).

A proton has the same **mass** as a neutron. The mass of an electron is **negligible** (nearly zero).

All atoms of the same element have the same number of protons.

(HT) You can use information from the periodic table to work out the number of protons, electrons and neutrons in any atom. For example, consider $^{19}_{9}F$. The atomic number is the number of protons. In this example, fluorine has nine protons. For the atom to be neutral, it must have the same number of electrons: nine. The mass of the atom is 19, and we know that only protons and neutrons have mass, so the rest of the mass (19 minus 9) must come from neutrons. So fluorine atoms have 10 neutrons.

Atomic Particle	Relative Mass	Relative Charge
Proton	1	+1
Neutron	1	0
Electron	Nearly zero	−1

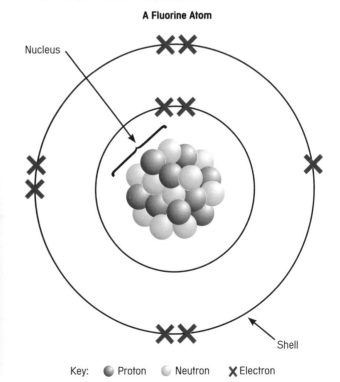

A Fluorine Atom

Nucleus

Shell

Key:　● Proton　● Neutron　✗ Electron

C4 Chemical Patterns

Spectroscopy

Some elements emit distinctive coloured flames when they're heated:

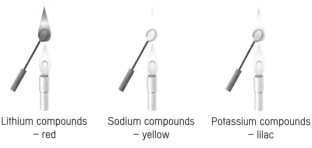

Lithium compounds – red   Sodium compounds – yellow   Potassium compounds – lilac

N.B. You don't need to remember these colours.

The light emitted from the flame of an element produces a characteristic **line spectrum**.

Scientists realised some time ago that each element has its own unique spectrum.

The study of **spectra** has been increasingly used to analyse unknown substances and discover new elements. For example, the line spectrum for helium was first seen in light from the Sun, before it was discovered on Earth.

Electron Configuration

The **electron configuration** of an atom shows how the electrons are arranged in shells around the **nucleus**:

- The electrons in an atom fill up the lowest energy level first. This is the shell closest to the nucleus.
- The first shell can hold up to two electrons.
- The shells after this can hold up to eight electrons.

An electron configuration is written as a series of numbers, e.g. 2.8.1. Going across a **period**, electron configurations increase by one, e.g. sodium 2.8.1, magnesium 2.8.2, aluminium 2.8.3, until the outer shell is full, e.g. argon 2.8.8.

N.B. This is only true for the first 20 elements.

The Electron Configurations of the First 20 Elements

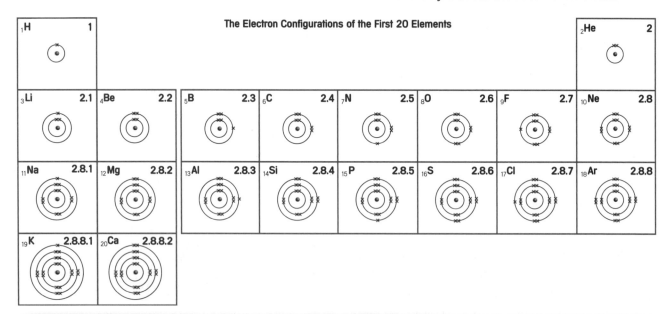

Quick Test

1. Why are lithium, sodium and potassium all found in the same group of the periodic table? Use ideas about their properties and their electron configurations.
2. What is the mass and charge of…
   (a) a proton?   **(b)** an electron?   **(c)** a neutron?

(HT) Balanced Equations

The total mass of the **products** of a chemical reaction is always equal to the total mass of the **reactants**. This is because **no atoms are lost or made**.

So, chemical symbol equations must always be **balanced**. There must be the same number of atoms of each element on both sides of the equation.

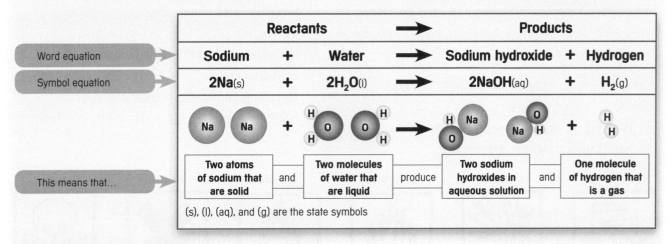

	Reactants			→		Products		
Word equation	Sodium	+	Water	→	Sodium hydroxide	+	Hydrogen	
Symbol equation	$2Na_{(s)}$	+	$2H_2O_{(l)}$	→	$2NaOH_{(aq)}$	+	$H_{2(g)}$	

This means that...	Two atoms of sodium that are solid	and	Two molecules of water that are liquid	produce	Two sodium hydroxides in aqueous solution	and	One molecule of hydrogen that is a gas

(s), (l), (aq), and (g) are the state symbols

Writing Balanced Equations

Follow these steps to write a balanced equation:

1. Write a word equation for the chemical reaction.
2. Substitute **formulae** for the names of the elements or **compounds** involved.
3. Balance the equation by adding numbers in front of the reactants and / or products.
4. Write a balanced symbol equation.

	Reactants			→	Products
1 Write a word equation	Magnesium	+	Oxygen	→	Magnesium oxide
2 Replace with formulae	Mg	+	O_2	→	MgO

3 Balance the equation

- There are two **O**s on the reactant side, but only one **O** on the product side. We need to add another **MgO** to the product side to balance the **O**s.
- We now need to add another **Mg** on the reactant side to balance the **Mg**s.
- There are two magnesium atoms and two oxygen atoms on each side – **it's balanced**.

4 Write the balanced symbol equation	$2Mg_{(s)}$	+	$O_{2(g)}$	→	$2MgO_{(s)}$

C4 Chemical Patterns

Hazardous Substances

Hazards are identified by **symbols** that have specific meanings. When using hazardous chemicals it's impossible to completely remove all of the risks. However, following accepted guidelines and taking sensible precautions can help to reduce the risk.

Common safety precautions for handling hazardous chemicals are as follows:

- Wearing gloves and eye protection, and washing hands after handling chemicals.
- Using safety screens.
- Using small amounts and low concentrations of the chemicals.
- Working in a fume cupboard or ventilating the room.
- Not eating or drinking when working with chemicals.
- Not using flammable substances near to naked flames.

Corrosive	Explosive	Flammable	Oxidising	Harmful	Toxic

Group 1 – The Alkali Metals

There are six metals in Group 1. They're called the **alkali metals**. The physical **properties** of the alkali metals alter as you go down the group. The further an **element** is down the group…

- the **higher** the **reactivity**
- the **lower** the **melting** and **boiling points**
- the higher the density.

Element	Melting Point (°C)	Boiling Point (°C)	Density (g/cm³)
Lithium, Li	180	1340	0.53
Sodium, Na	98	883	0.97
Potassium, K	64	760	0.86
Rubidium, Rb	39	688	1.53
Caesium, Cs	29	671	1.90

(HT) Trends in Group 1

Alkali metals have similar properties because they all have **one electron** in their outer shell.

The alkali metals become **more reactive** as you go down the group because the outer shell gets further away from the influence of the **nucleus** and so the outer electron is **lost more easily**.

Lithium Atom 2.1	Sodium Atom 2.8.1	Potassium Atom 2.8.8.1

More reactive →

Alkali Metal Compounds

Alkali metals can react to form **compounds**.

Alkali metals are shiny when freshly cut, but they quickly **tarnish in moist air**, go dull and become covered in a layer of metal oxide.

Alkali metals react **vigorously** with **chlorine** to form white crystalline **salts**.

A general equation can be used, where M refers to the alkali metal:

$$2M_{(s)} + Cl_{2(g)} \longrightarrow 2MCl_{(s)}$$

For example:

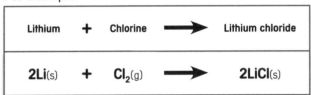

Lithium + Chlorine → Lithium chloride

$$2Li_{(s)} + Cl_{2(g)} \longrightarrow 2LiCl_{(s)}$$

Alkali metals react with **water** to form a **metal hydroxide** and **hydrogen gas**. The metal hydroxide dissolves in water to form an **alkaline** solution:

$$2M_{(s)} + 2H_2O_{(l)} \longrightarrow 2MOH_{(aq)} + H_{2(g)}$$

N.B. (s) means solid; (l) means liquid; (g) means gas; (aq) means aqueous (dissolved in water)

For example:

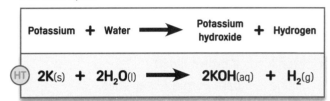

Potassium + Water → Potassium hydroxide + Hydrogen

(HT) $$2K_{(s)} + 2H_2O_{(l)} \longrightarrow 2KOH_{(aq)} + H_{2(g)}$$

When lithium, sodium and potassium react with cold water they...
- float (due to their low density)
- produce bubbles of hydrogen gas.

The reactivity of alkali metals increases further down the group:
- Lithium reacts quickly with water.
- Sodium reacts more vigorously with water and melts.
- Potassium reacts so vigorously with water that sparks are produced and a purple flame is seen.

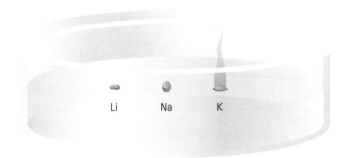

Li   Na   K

Hazards of Alkali Metals

Alkali metals carry hazard symbols. When working with Group 1 metals, you should...
- use small amounts of the metals
- wear safety glasses and use safety screens
- watch teacher demonstrations carefully
- avoid working near naked flames
- ensure that the metals are stored under oil and that the lids are always tightly secured.

Quick Test

1. Describe the trends in melting point and reactivity as you go down Group 1.
2. Give one reason why the Group 1 elements are called 'alkali metals'.
3. Describe how potassium reacts with cold water.
4. (HT) Why does potassium react faster than sodium?

C4 Chemical Patterns

Group 7 – The Halogens

There are five non-metals in Group 7.

At room temperature and room pressure...
- chlorine is a **green gas**
- bromine is a **brown liquid**
- iodine is a **dark purple / grey solid**.

N.B. Iodine turns into a purple gas when heated.

All **halogens** consist of **diatomic molecules** (they only exist in pairs of **atoms**), e.g. Cl_2, Br_2, I_2.

You can use halogens to **bleach dyes** and **kill bacteria** in water. The physical **properties** of the halogens alter as you go down the group.

The further an element is down the group...
- the **lower** the **reactivity**
- the **higher** the **melting** and **boiling points**
- the **higher** the **density**.

Halogens react with alkali metals to produce **halides**.

Here are some examples:

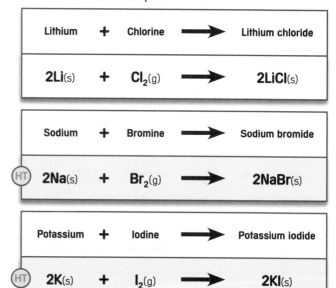

| Lithium | + | Chlorine | → | Lithium chloride |
| **2Li**(s) | + | **Cl$_2$**(g) | → | **2LiCl**(s) |

| Sodium | + | Bromine | → | Sodium bromide |
| (HT) **2Na**(s) | + | **Br$_2$**(g) | → | **2NaBr**(s) |

| Potassium | + | Iodine | → | Potassium iodide |
| (HT) **2K**(s) | + | **I$_2$**(g) | → | **2KI**(s) |

Halogen	Melting Point (°C)	Boiling Point (°C)	Density (g/cm³)
Fluorine, F_2	-220	-188	0.0016
Chlorine, Cl_2	-101	-34	0.003
Bromine, Br_2	-7	59	3.12
Iodine, I_2	114	184	4.95
Astatine, At_2	302 (estimated)	337 (estimated)	Not known

(HT) Trends in Group 7

The halogens have similar properties because they all have **seven electrons** in their outer shell.

The halogens become **less reactive** as you go down the group because the outer shell gets further away from the influence of the **nucleus** and so an electron is **less easily gained**.

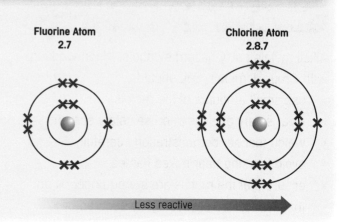

Fluorine Atom
2.7

Chlorine Atom
2.8.7

Less reactive

Halogen • Diatomic molecule • Atom

Hazards of Halogens

Halogens carry hazard symbols.

When working with halogens, you should…
- wear safety glasses
- work in a fume cupboard
- make sure the room is well ventilated
- use small amounts of very dilute concentrations
- avoid working near naked flames
- watch teacher demonstrations carefully.

Halogen	Hazard Symbol		
Fluorine, F_2	☠	🔥	⚗
Chlorine, Cl_2	☠	🔥	
Bromine, Br_2	☠	⚗	
Iodine, I_2	✖	🔥	

Displacement Reactions of Halogens

A **more reactive** halogen will **displace** a **less reactive** halogen from an aqueous solution of its salt. This means that chlorine will displace both bromine and iodine, while bromine will displace iodine.

An example is shown opposite.

Potassium iodide + Chlorine ⟶ Potassium chloride + Iodine

$$2KI_{(aq)} + Cl_{2(aq)} \longrightarrow 2KCl_{(aq)} + I_{2(aq)}$$

Reactions of Halogens with Alkali Metals

Halogens react with other elements to form **compounds**.

Their reactions with alkali metals are highly **exothermic**. They form ionic compounds. An example is shown opposite.

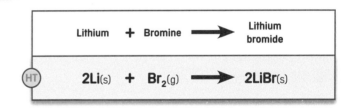

Lithium + Bromine ⟶ Lithium bromide

HT $$2Li_{(s)} + Br_{2(g)} \longrightarrow 2LiBr_{(s)}$$

Properties of the Compounds of Halogens with Alkali Metals

Experiments show that **compounds** of alkali metals and halogens **conduct electricity** when they're molten or dissolved in water.

You can conclude from this that they're made up of **charged particles** called **ions**.

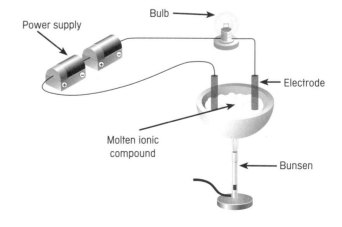

Power supply

Bulb

Electrode

Molten ionic compound

Bunsen

C4 Chemical Patterns

Ions

Ions are atoms (or groups of atoms) that have gained or lost electrons.

As the numbers of protons and electrons are no longer equal, ions have an overall charge.

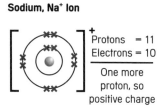

Sodium, Na Atom

Protons = 11
Electrons = 11

Equal number of protons and electrons, so no charge

Sodium, Na⁺ Ion

Protons = 11
Electrons = 10

One more proton, so positive charge

Ionic Bonding

Ionic bonding occurs between a metal and a non-metal. Electrons transfer from one atom to another to form electrically charged ions:

- Atoms that lose electrons become positively charged ions.
- Atoms that gain electrons become negatively charged ions.

Each ion has a full or empty outer shell of electrons.

Compounds of Group 1 metals and Group 7 elements are ionic compounds (salts). Ionic compounds form crystals because the ions are arranged into a regular lattice. When ionic crystals melt or dissolve in water, they conduct electricity.

Ionic compounds conduct electricity when they're molten or dissolved in water because the charged ions are free to move around.

Ionic Lattice

+ Positively charged ion

- Negatively charged ion

Example 1 – Sodium Chloride

Sodium and chlorine bond ionically to form sodium chloride, NaCl:

1. The sodium (Na) atom has one electron in its outer shell that is transferred to the chlorine (Cl) atom.
2. The sodium (Na) atom has lost one electron and is now a positively charged sodium ion (Na⁺). The chlorine (Cl) atom has gained one electron and is now a negatively charged chloride ion (Cl⁻).
3. Both atoms now have eight electrons in their outer shell. The atoms become ions Na⁺ and Cl⁻ and the compound formed is sodium chloride, NaCl.

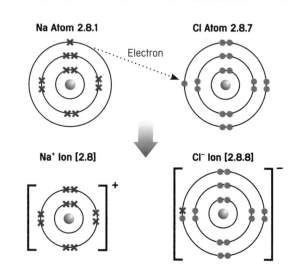

Na Atom 2.8.1   Cl Atom 2.8.7

Electron

Na⁺ Ion [2.8]   Cl⁻ Ion [2.8.8]

Example 2 – Potassium Chloride

Potassium and chlorine bond ionically to form potassium chloride, KCl:

1. The potassium (K) atom has one electron in its outer shell that is transferred to the chlorine (Cl) atom.
2. The potassium (K) atom has lost one electron and is now a positively charged potassium ion (K^+). The chlorine (Cl) atom has gained one electron and is now a negatively charged chloride ion (Cl^-).
3. Both atoms now have **eight electrons in their outer shell**. The compound formed is potassium chloride, KCl.

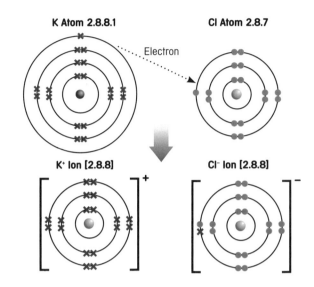

HT Formulae of Ionic Compounds

Ionic compounds are electrically **neutral** substances that have equal amounts of positive and negative charge.

If you know the charge given on both ions you can work out the formula.

For example, Na^+ and Cl^- combine to form NaCl.

If you know the formula and the charge on one of the ions, you can work out the charge on the other ion.

For example, $MgBr_2$ is made up of two Br^- ions that combine with one Mg^{2+} ion.

		Negative Ions	
		1– e.g. Cl^-, OH^-	2– e.g. SO_4^{2-}, O^{2-}
Positive Ions	1+ e.g. K^+, Na^+	KCl 1+ ↙ ↘ 1–	K_2SO_4 2 × 1+ = 2+ ↙ ↘ 2–
		NaOH 1+ ↙ ↘ 1–	Na_2O 2 × 1+ = 2+ ↙ ↘ 2–
	2+ e.g. Mg^{2+}, Cu^{2+}	$MgCl_2$ 2+ ↙ ↘ 2 × 1– = 2–	$MgSO_4$ 2+ ↙ ↘ 2–
		$Cu(OH)_2$ 2+ ↙ ↘ 2 × 1– = 2–	CuO 2+ ↙ ↘ 2–
	3+ e.g. Al^{3+}, Fe^{3+}	$AlCl_3$ 3+ ↙ ↘ 3 × 1– = 3–	$Al_2(SO_4)_3$ 2 × 3+ = 6+ ↙ ↘ 3 × 2– = 6–
		$Fe(OH)_3$ 3+ ↙ ↘ 3 × 1– = 3–	Fe_2O_3 2 × 3+ = 6+ ↙ ↘ 3 × 2– = 6–

Quick Test

1. Which of these is the odd one out and why? Chlorine; lithium; iodine; bromine; fluorine.
2. What happens to the melting point and reactivity of the halogens as you go down the group?
3. What will be the products when bromine is mixed with a solution of potassium iodide?
4. What is the name of the product made when lithium reacts with fluorine?

1 **(a)** Complete the table below about sub-atomic particles. [3]

Particle	Relative Mass	Relative Charge
....	1	....
Neutron	....	....
....	Negligible	....

(b) Complete the labels on the diagram below. [2]

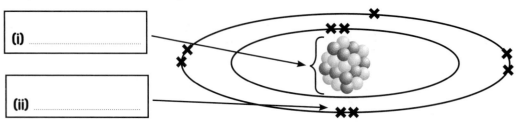

(i) ....

(ii) ....

(c) Define the term **atomic number**. [1]

(d) Sophie, Catherine and Imran are discussing their understanding of the halogen elements in Group 7 of the periodic table.

Sophie
All of the halogen elements are gases at room temperature.

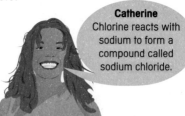

Catherine
Chlorine reacts with sodium to form a compound called sodium chloride.

Imran
The halogens react in similar ways because they all have seven electrons in their outer shell.

(i) Which of the students is **incorrect**? Put a ring around the appropriate answer. [1]

Sophie **Catherine** **Imran**

(ii) Write a word equation for the reaction that Catherine is describing. [2]

2 This question is about the elements in Group 1 of the periodic table.

(a) What name is given to the elements in Group 1? [1]

(b) Use your knowledge and understanding of the properties of the elements in Group 1 to complete the following table. [3]

Element	Melting Point (K)	Boiling Point (K)	Formula of Chloride
Lithium	453	....	LiCl
Sodium	370	1156	....
Potassium	....	1032	KCl

(c) Describe what happens when a piece of sodium is placed in a large bowl of water. Include a word equation for the reaction that occurs and state the pH of the solution that is formed. **[4]**

....

....

....

....

(d) The following hazard symbol is found on a jar containing sodium. State what it means and describe a safety precaution that you would follow when dealing with any chemical that has this hazard symbol. **[2]**

....

....

HT **3** This question is about the element fluorine.

(a) Work out the number of protons, electrons and neutrons in an atom of fluorine. **[3]**

Protons: .... Electrons: .... Neutrons: ....

(b) Fluorine is a diatomic gas and has the formula F_2. Write a balanced symbol equation for the reaction between fluorine and sodium, including state symbols. **[3]**

....

(c) A student places some solid lead fluoride powder into a beaker and then places two electrodes into the solid to see if it conducts electricity. The electrodes are connected in series to a power pack and a lamp that will light if the lead fluoride conducts electricity. After making her first observation, the solid lead fluoride is heated strongly until it melts. The power pack is left switched on throughout the experiment. Describe and explain what the student will see. **[6]**

✎ *The quality of written communication will be assessed in your answer to this question.*

....

....

....

....

....

....

....

....

C5 Chemicals of the Natural Environment

The Earth's Resources

The Earth is made up of different parts.

The **atmosphere** is a layer of gas surrounding the Earth. It's made up of…
* the **elements** nitrogen, oxygen and argon
* some **compounds** (e.g. carbon dioxide and water vapour).

The **hydrosphere** is mostly made up of water and some dissolved compounds.

The **lithosphere** is the rigid outer layer of the Earth, made up of the crust and the part of the mantle just below it. It consists of a mixture of minerals (e.g. silicon dioxide), and an abundance of the elements silicon, oxygen and aluminium.

Chemicals of the Atmosphere

Dry atmospheric air is made from 78% nitrogen, 21% oxygen, nearly 1% argon and approximately 0.04% carbon dioxide.

The chemicals that make up the atmosphere consist of…
* non-metal elements
* molecular compounds made up from non-metal elements.

From the table below, you can see that the molecules (with the exception of water) that make up the atmosphere are gases at 20°C because they have low boiling points. This can be explained by looking at the structure of the molecules:
* Gases have small molecules **with weak forces of attraction between them**.
* Only small amounts of energy are needed to break these forces.

Pure molecular compounds don't conduct electricity because their molecules aren't charged.

HT The atoms within molecules are connected by strong **covalent bonds**. In a covalent bond…
* the **electrons** are shared between the **atoms**.
* a strong, **electrostatic attraction** is created between each positive nucleus and the shared pair of negative electrons.

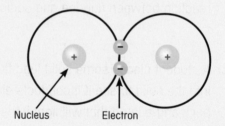

Nucleus   Electron

Chemical	2D Molecular Diagram	3D Molecular Diagram	Melting Point (°C)	Boiling Point (°C)
Oxygen, O_2	O=O		-218	-183
Nitrogen, N_2	N≡N		-210	-196
Carbon dioxide, CO_2	O=C=O		Sublimes (no liquid state)	-78
Water vapour, H_2O	H–O–H		0	100
Argon, Ar	Ar		-189	-186

Key Words   Atmosphere • Element • Compound • Hydrosphere • Lithosphere

Chemicals of the Lithosphere

The **lithosphere** is made from the crust and the part of the mantle just below it.

This table shows the abundance of some of the **elements** in the Earth's crust. For example, you can see that the three most abundant elements are…

- oxygen
- silicon
- aluminium.

N.B. You may be asked to interpret data like this in your exam.

Element	Abundance in Lithosphere (ppm)
Oxygen, O	455 000
Silicon, Si	272 000
Aluminium, Al	83 000
Iron, Fe	62 000
Calcium, Ca	46 600
Magnesium, Mg	27 640
Sodium, Na	22 700
Potassium, K	18 400
Titanium, Ti	6320
Hydrogen, H	1520
Carbon, C	940

Carbon in the Lithosphere

Diamond and **graphite** are both minerals formed from pure carbon that is found in the lithosphere.

You can see from the diagrams that in diamond, each carbon atom is covalently bonded to four other carbon atoms. This explains why diamond is very hard.

The diagram of graphite shows that each carbon atom is covalently bonded to three other carbon atoms and that they're arranged in sheets that can slide easily over each other. This explains why graphite is soft. Spare electrons can move between the layers of atoms, so graphite can conduct electricity.

In both graphite and diamond, the covalent bonds are strong, so they both have high melting points and are insoluble in water.

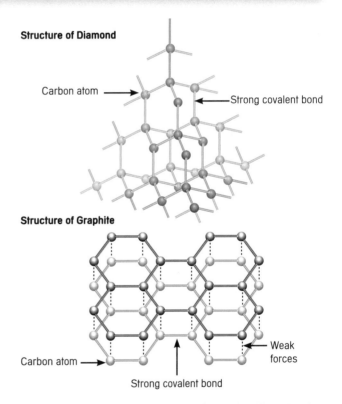

Structure of Diamond

Carbon atom ⟶
Strong covalent bond ⟵

Structure of Graphite

Carbon atom ⟶
Strong covalent bond
Weak forces ⟵

Silicon Dioxide in the Lithosphere

A lot of the silicon and oxygen in the lithosphere is present as the compound silicon dioxide (SiO_2).

Silicon dioxide forms a giant covalent structure, so it has similar properties to diamond.

Silicon dioxide has the following properties:
- Hard
- High melting point
- Electrical insulator
- Insoluble in water.

C5 Chemicals of the Natural Environment

Chemicals of the Hydrosphere

Seawater in the **hydrosphere** is 'salty' because it contains dissolved **ionic compounds** called **salts**.

For example, sodium chloride is an ionic compound made from positive sodium **ions** and negative chloride ions. The ions are **electrostatically attracted** to each other to form a **giant 3D crystal lattice** with high melting and boiling points.

HT If given a table of charges on **ions**, you need to be able to work out the **formulae for salts** in the sea.

For example, you should be able to work out the formulae for sodium chloride, magnesium sulfate, potassium chloride and potassium bromide. This was covered in Module C4.

Properties of Ionic Compounds

Ionic compounds have similar properties: high melting points; they don't conduct electricity when solid; they do conduct electricity when molten or dissolved. Chemists developed an explanation of the structure of ionic compounds to explain these properties:

- They have high melting and boiling points because the ions are held together by strong forces of attraction in a lattice (see page 42).

- They don't conduct electricity when solid because the ions are fixed in place and can't move.
- They conduct electricity when molten (or dissolved) because the ions are free to move.

Many ionic compounds dissolve in water because the water molecules are polar (have a positive end and a negative end):

1 A water molecule is attracted to an ion in the crystal lattice.	**2** An ion breaks away from the lattice.	**3** The ion moves freely through the water.
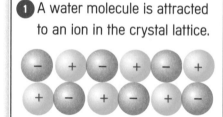	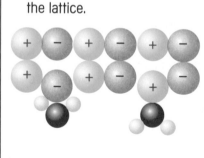	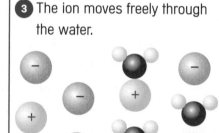

Quick Test

1. What is meant by the term 'hydrosphere'?
2. What is the percentage of oxygen in dry air?
3. State two properties of diamond.
4. State two typical properties of ionic compounds.

Using Precipitation to Test for Ions

In the oceans calcium ions (Ca^{2+}) combine with carbonate ions (CO_3^{2-}) to form the **insoluble** ionic compound calcium carbonate ($CaCO_3$), or limestone. Insoluble solids formed in these types of reaction are called **precipitates**. We can use **precipitation** reactions to detect ions in aqueous solutions.

We can make predictions about precipitation reactions by interpreting information on solubility. For example, if we know that magnesium carbonate is insoluble, then mixing a solution that contains magnesium ions (e.g. magnesium chloride) with a solution that contains carbonate ions (e.g. sodium carbonate) will result in the precipitation of insoluble magnesium carbonate.

Testing for Metal Ions

Many positive metal ions can be identified in solution by adding sodium hydroxide solution (NaOH) and observing the colour of the precipitate.

You can see some of the results in the table. You don't need to learn the colours but you will be expected to interpret results tables in the exam.

Metal Ion Present	Colour of Precipitate When NaOH Added
Cu^{2+}	Light blue
Fe^{2+}	Green
Fe^{3+}	Red-brown

HT We know that the hydroxide ion has a single negative charge (OH^-). This means that we can work out the formula of the metal hydroxide produced and write a balanced ionic equation. Look at these examples:

$$Cu^{2+}{(aq)} + 2OH^-{(aq)} \longrightarrow Cu(OH)_2{(s)}$$

$$Fe^{3+}{(aq)} + 3OH^-{(aq)} \longrightarrow Fe(OH)_3{(s)}$$

You need two hydroxide ions to balance the charge on the Cu^{2+} ion, but three to balance the charge on the Fe^{3+} ion. Notice how this allows you to work out the formula of the metal hydroxide produced.

Testing for Negative Ions

Many negative (non-metal) ions can be identified in solution because they will react with other aqueous ions to produce an insoluble precipitate. Here are some examples:

Ion	Add	Observe	**HT** Ionic Equation
Chloride, Cl^-	$AgNO_3{(aq)}$	White precipitate	$Ag^+{(aq)} + Cl^-{(aq)} \longrightarrow AgCl{(s)}$
Bromide, Br^-	$AgNO_3{(aq)}$	Cream precipitate	$Ag^+{(aq)} + Br^-{(aq)} \longrightarrow AgBr{(s)}$
Iodide, I^-	$AgNO_3{(aq)}$	Yellow precipitate	$Ag^+{(aq)} + I^-{(aq)} \longrightarrow AgI{(s)}$
Sulfate, SO_4^{2-}	$Ba(NO_3)_2{(aq)}$	White precipitate	$Ba^{2+}{(aq)} + SO_4^{2-}{(aq)} \longrightarrow BaSO_4{(s)}$

Key Words   Precipitate • Precipitation

C5 Chemicals of the Natural Environment

Extracting Useful Metals

Ores are rocks that contain varying amounts of **minerals**, from which **metals** can be extracted.

Sometimes very large amounts of ores need to be mined in order to recover a small percentage of valuable minerals, for example, copper.

The method of extraction depends on how reactive the metal is.

Metals that are less reactive than carbon (e.g. zinc, iron and copper) can be extracted from their oxides by heating with carbon:

- The metal oxide is **reduced**, as it has lost oxygen.
- The carbon is **oxidised**, as it has gained oxygen.

For example, zinc can be extracted from zinc oxide by heating it with carbon:

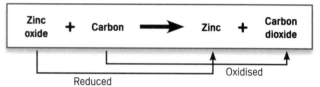

Relative Formula Mass

The **relative formula mass (RFM)** tells you the total mass of the atoms in a compound. All you have to do is add up the relative atomic masses (RAMs) that you can find on the periodic table. Here are two examples:

- The RFM of CO_2 is $12 + 16 + 16 = 44$
- The RFM of $CaCO_3$ is $40 + 12 + 16 + 16 + 16 = 100$
  (So in 100g of $CaCO_3$, 40g is calcium.)

$$^{12}_{6}C$$ Relative atomic mass of carbon is 12

$$^{40}_{20}Ca$$ Relative atomic mass of calcium is 40

$$^{16}_{8}O$$ Relative atomic mass of oxygen is 16

HT Calculating a Metal's Mass

If you're given its formula, you can calculate the mass of metal that can be extracted from a substance:

1. Write down the formula.
2. Work out the relative formula mass.
3. Work out the percentage mass of the metal.
4. Work out the mass of the metal.

Example

Find the mass of Zn that can be extracted from 100g of ZnO.

1. ZnO
2. Relative formula mass $= 65 + 16 = 81$
3. Percentage of zinc present
   $$= \frac{\text{RAM of Zn}}{\text{RFM of ZnO}} \times 100 = \frac{65}{81} \times 100 = 80\%$$
4. In 100g of ZnO, there will be $\frac{80}{100} \times 100$
   $$= \textbf{80g of Zn}$$

If you were given the equation of a reaction, you could find the ratio of the mass of the reactant to the mass of the product.

$$2ZnO_{(s)} \: + \: C_{(s)} \longrightarrow 2Zn_{(s)} \: + \: CO_{2(g)}$$

Relative formula mass:

Work out the RFM of each substance

$$(2 \times 81) + 12 = (2 \times 65) + 44$$
$$162 + 12 = 130 + 44$$
$$174 = 174$$

Therefore, 162g of ZnO produces 130g of Zn.

So, 1g of ZnO $= \frac{130}{162} = 0.8g$ of Zn

and 100g of ZnO $= 0.8 \times 100 = \textbf{80g of Zn}$

Electrolysis

Electrolysis is the breaking down of an **electrolyte** using an **electric current**.

The process is used to extract **reactive metals** from their ores because they're too reactive to be extracted by heating with carbon.

Ionic compounds conduct electricity when they're...

*   molten
*   dissolved in solution.

This is because their **ions** are free to move through the liquid.

When an ionic compound melts, electrostatic forces between the charged ions in the crystal lattice are broken down and the ions are free to move.

Electrolysis

Negative electrode −

Positive electrode +

When a direct current is passed through a molten ionic compound...

*   positively charged ions are attracted towards the **negative electrode**
*   negatively charged ions are attracted towards the **positive electrode**.

For example, in the electrolysis of molten lead bromide...

*   positively charged lead ions are attracted towards the **negative electrode**, forming lead (a metal)
*   negatively charged bromide ions are attracted towards the **positive electrode**, forming bromine (a non-metal).

(HT) When ions get to the oppositely charged electrode they're **discharged**, i.e. they lose their charge.

For example, in the electrolysis of molten lead bromide the non-metal ion loses electrons to the positive electrode to form a bromine atom. The bromine atom then bonds with a second atom to form a bromine molecule.

The reactions at the electrodes can be written as **half equations**. This means that you write separate equations for what is happening at each of the electrodes during electrolysis.

$$2Br^- \longrightarrow Br_2 + 2e^-$$

The lead ions gain electrons from the negative electrode to form a lead atom:

$$Pb^{2+} + 2e^- \longrightarrow Pb$$

This process completes the circuit as the electrons are exchanged at the electrodes.

C5 Chemicals of the Natural Environment

Extracting Aluminium by Electrolysis

Aluminium is extracted from its **ore** by **electrolysis**:

1. Aluminium ore (bauxite) is purified to leave aluminium oxide.
2. Aluminium oxide is mixed with cryolite (a compound of aluminium) to lower its melting point.
3. The mixture of aluminium oxide and cryolite is melted, so that the **ions** can move.
4. When a **current** passes through the molten mixture, positively charged aluminium ions move towards the **negative electrode**.
5. Aluminium is formed at the negative electrode.
6. Negatively charged oxide ions move towards the **positive electrode**.
7. Oxygen is formed at the positive electrode.

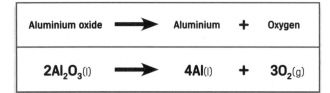

Aluminium oxide	$\longrightarrow$	Aluminium	+	Oxygen
$2Al_2O_{3(l)}$	$\longrightarrow$	$4Al_{(l)}$	+	$3O_{2(g)}$

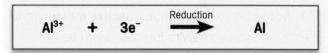 At the negative electrode, aluminium ions gain electrons to become neutral atoms:

$$Al^{3+} + 3e^- \xrightarrow{\text{Reduction}} Al$$

At the positive electrode, oxygen ions lose electrons to become neutral atoms:

$$2O^{2-} - 4e^- \xrightarrow{\text{Oxidation}} O_2$$

This can also be written as:

$$2O^{2-} \longrightarrow O_2 + 4e^-$$

Metals and the Environment

This table shows the **environmental impacts** of extracting, using and disposing of metals.

A life cycle assessment helps scientists to make decisions about which method of extraction causes the least environmental damage.

Stage of Life Cycle	Process	Environmental Impact
Making the material from natural raw materials	Mining	• Lots of rock wasted. • Leaves a scar on the landscape. • Air / noise pollution.
	Processing	• Pollutants caused by transportation. • Energy usage. • Electrolysis uses more energy than reduction.
Manufacture	Manufacturing metal products	• Energy usage in processing and transportation.
Use	Transport to shops / home	• Pollutants caused by transportation.
	Running the product	• Energy usage.
Disposal	Reuse	• No impact.
	Recycle	• Uses a lot less energy than the initial manufacturing.
	Throw away	• Landfill sites remove wildlife habitats and are an eyesore.

Chemicals of the Natural Environment C5

Properties of Metals

A metal has a **giant structure** of **ions** that is held together by a strong force of attraction called the **metallic bond**. Metals…

- are **strong** – the ions are closely packed in a lattice structure
- have **high melting points** – a lot of energy is needed to break the strong metallic bonds.

(HT) Metals are also…

- **malleable** – they can be beaten into shape or dented as the layers of metal ions can slide over each other
- **conductors of electricity** – electrons are free to move throughout the structure. When a voltage is applied, the electrons move through the metal in one direction.

In a metal, the positively charged metal ions are held strongly together by a **'sea' of electrons**.

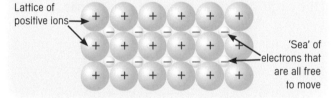

Lattice of positive ions

'Sea' of electrons that are all free to move

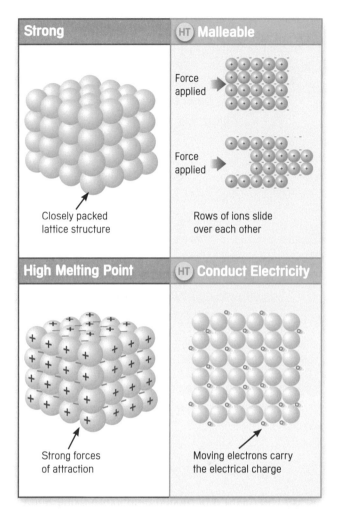

Strong	(HT) Malleable
Closely packed lattice structure	Force applied — Force applied — Rows of ions slide over each other

High Melting Point	(HT) Conduct Electricity
Strong forces of attraction	Moving electrons carry the electrical charge

Uses of Metals

The properties of metals determine how they're used:

- Titanium is **strong** and is used for replacement hip joints and submarines.
- Aluminium is **malleable** and is used for drinks cans.
- Iron has a **high melting point** and is used for making saucepans.
- Copper is an excellent **conductor** of electricity and is used for cables and electrical switches.

Quick Test

1. Describe how you would test for a metal ion in an aqueous solution.
2. Describe how you would test for the presence of sulfate ions.
3. What happens to the positive and negative ions in electrolysis?
4. Name the products at the positive and negative electrodes in the electrolysis of aluminium oxide.
5. (HT) Write a balanced ionic equation to show the formation of iron(III) hydroxide, $Fe(OH)_3$, from iron(III) ions (Fe^{3+}) and hydroxide ions (OH^-).

1 Waste water from a chemical factory must be processed to remove any ions that might cause pollution. Some ions are harmless but others are dangerous for plants and animals. The water from the chemical plant is regularly tested to ensure that it's safe to be released into the nearby river. The data sheet on page 112 shows the tests that are carried out to detect some of the ions in the water.

(a) Gemma is an analytical chemist working at the plant. She suspects that the water from the factory has been contaminated with copper(II) chloride. Describe two tests that she should carry out to confirm her hypothesis and state the results that she should expect to observe. **[4]**

....

....

....

....

(b) On another day, Gemma adds dilute hydrochloric acid to a water sample and observes bubbles. Identify the negative ion present in the water and name the gas produced. **[2]**

....

....

2 (a) Aluminium oxide powder is mixed with a substance called cryolite. The mixture is then melted. Describe what happens to the aluminium ions and the oxide ions when aluminium oxide melts. **[2]**

....

....

(b) The mixture of molten aluminium oxide and cryolite is then electrolysed. The diagram below shows this happening.

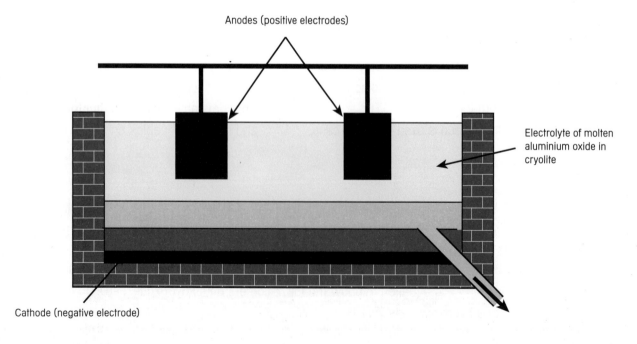

Anodes (positive electrodes)

Electrolyte of molten aluminium oxide in cryolite

Cathode (negative electrode)

Use the words provided to complete the following sentences. You can use words once, more than once, or not at all. **[2]**

nitrogen	oxygen	bottom	top	aluminium	cathode

Aluminium oxide breaks down into _____ and aluminium when the current flows through the molten aluminium oxide.

The aluminium metal forms at the _____ of the cell, where it's siphoned off.

The _____ gas is produced at the _____ of the cell, at the carbon anodes.

(c) Aluminium has several uses, including saucepans, power lines and aeroplanes. State which properties of aluminium are important for each of these uses and use your understanding of metallic bonding to explain why aluminium has these properties. **[6]**

✎ *The quality of written communication will be assessed in your answer to this question.*

_____

_____

_____

_____

_____

_____

_____

_____

HT **3** **(a)** Many metal ions can be detected in solution by precipitation. Zinc ions can be detected by adding carbonate ions (CO_3^{2-}) to form the insoluble compound zinc carbonate ($ZnCO_3$). Work out the charge on the zinc ion and then write a balanced ionic equation, including state symbols. **[3]**

_____

_____

(b) Copper ions (Cu^{2+}) can be detected using a solution of sodium hydroxide, which contains hydroxide ions (OH^-). Write a balanced ionic equation, including state symbols, to show the formation of the insoluble copper(II) hydroxide. **[3]**

C6 Chemical Synthesis

Chemicals

Chemical synthesis is the process by which raw materials are made into useful products including…
- food additives
- fertilisers
- dyestuffs
- pigments
- pharmaceuticals
- paints.

The chemical industry makes **bulk chemicals** on a very large scale and **fine chemicals** on a much smaller scale.

The range of chemicals made in industry and laboratories in the UK is illustrated in this pie chart:

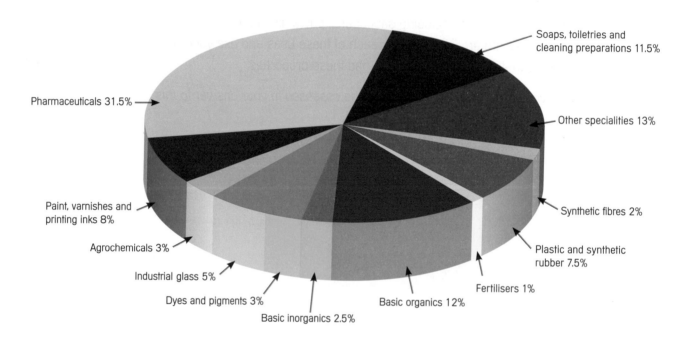

Pharmaceuticals 31.5%

Soaps, toiletries and cleaning preparations 11.5%

Other specialities 13%

Synthetic fibres 2%

Plastic and synthetic rubber 7.5%

Fertilisers 1%

Basic organics 12%

Basic inorganics 2.5%

Dyes and pigments 3%

Industrial glass 5%

Agrochemicals 3%

Paint, varnishes and printing inks 8%

Hazards

Many chemicals are **hazardous**, so it's important that you can…
- recognise the main hazard symbols
- understand the safety precautions to use.

Some examples of safety precautions are…
- wearing gloves and eye protection
- using safety screens
- not eating or drinking when working with chemicals
- not using flammable chemicals near to naked flames.

Corrosive

Explosive

Flammable

Oxidising

Harmful

Toxic

The pH Scale

The **pH scale** is a measure of the acidity or alkalinity of an **aqueous solution** across a 14-point scale:

- **Acids** are substances that have a pH less than 7.
- Bases are the oxides and hydroxides of metals. Soluble bases are called **alkalis** and have a pH greater than 7.

You can detect an acid or alkali using litmus paper.

You can measure the pH of a substance using an **indicator**, for example, universal indicator solution or a **pH meter**.

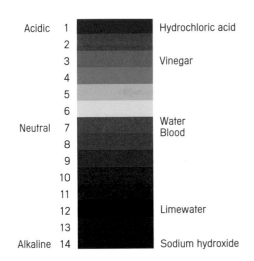

Acidic	1	Hydrochloric acid
	2	
	3	Vinegar
	4	
	5	
	6	
Neutral	7	Water
	8	Blood
	9	
	10	
	11	
	12	Limewater
	13	
Alkaline	14	Sodium hydroxide

Acidic Compounds

Acidic compounds produce aqueous **hydrogen ions**, $H^+(aq)$, when they dissolve in water.

Common Acids	Formulae to Remember	State at Room Temp.
Citric acid	–	Solid
Tartaric acid	–	Solid
Nitric acid	HNO_3	Liquid
Sulfuric acid	H_2SO_4	Liquid
Ethanoic acid	–	Liquid
Hydrogen chloride (hydrochloric acid)	HCl	Gas (or aqueous)

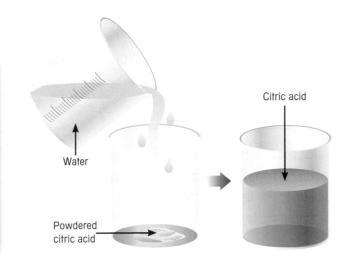

Water

Powdered citric acid

Citric acid

Alkali Compounds

Alkali compounds produce aqueous **hydroxide ions**, $OH^-(aq)$, when they dissolve in water.

Common Alkalis	Formulae to Remember
Sodium hydroxide	NaOH
Potassium hydroxide	–
Magnesium hydroxide	$Mg(OH)_2$
Calcium hydroxide	–

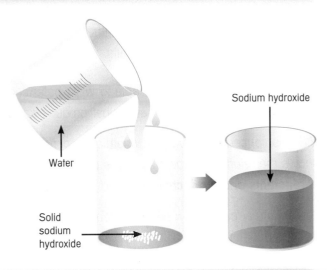

Water

Solid sodium hydroxide

Sodium hydroxide

C6 Chemical Synthesis

Neutralisation

When you mix together an **acid** and an **alkali** in the correct amounts they 'cancel out' each other.

Acid	+	Base	→	Salt	+	Water

This type of reaction is called **neutralisation**.

The **hydrogen ions** from the **acid** react with the **hydroxide ions** from the **alkali** to make water:

$$H^+_{(aq)} + OH^-_{(aq)} \longrightarrow H_2O_{(l)}$$

For example, hydrochloric acid and potassium hydroxide can be neutralised:

Hydrochloric acid	+	Potassium hydroxide	→	Potassium chloride	+	Water

$$HCl_{(aq)} + KOH_{(aq)} \longrightarrow KCl_{(aq)} + H_2O_{(l)}$$

Neutralising Hydrochloric Acid (HCl) and Potassium Hydroxide (KOH)

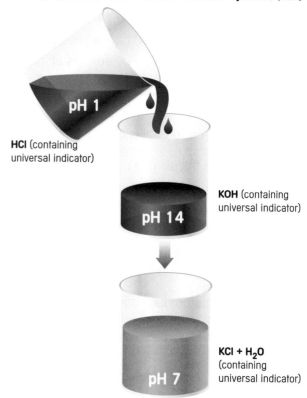

pH 1

HCl (containing universal indicator)

KOH (containing universal indicator)

pH 14

KCl + H₂O (containing universal indicator)

pH 7

Making Salts

Acids react with metal hydroxides, metal oxides and metal carbonates to form a salt and water. When an acid reacts with a metal carbonate, it also produces carbon dioxide.

Acids react with metals to form a salt and hydrogen.

The type of salt produced depends on the acid used:

- Hydro**chlor**ic acid produces **chloride** salts.
- **Sulf**uric acid produces **sulfate** salts.
- **Nitr**ic acid produces **nitrate** salts.

(HT) You need to know, and be able to write balanced equations for, the reactions of acids that produce salts.

*N.B. A balanced equation for a chemical reaction shows the relative numbers of **atoms** and molecules of **reactants** and **products** taking part in the reaction.*

You should already know how to balance equations that are unbalanced.

Hydrochloric acid	+	Sodium hydroxide	→	Sodium chloride	+	Water

$$HCl_{(aq)} + NaOH_{(aq)} \longrightarrow NaCl_{(aq)} + H_2O_{(l)}$$

Hydrochloric acid	+	Copper oxide	→	Copper chloride	+	Water

$$2HCl_{(aq)} + CuO_{(s)} \longrightarrow CuCl_{2(aq)} + H_2O_{(l)}$$

Hydrochloric acid	+	Calcium carbonate	→	Calcium chloride	+	Water	+	Carbon dioxide

$$2HCl_{(aq)} + CaCO_{3(s)} \longrightarrow CaCl_{2(aq)} + H_2O_{(l)} + CO_{2(g)}$$

Hydrochloric acid	+	Magnesium	→	Magnesium chloride	+	Hydrogen

$$2HCl_{(aq)} + Mg_{(s)} \longrightarrow MgCl_{2(aq)} + H_{2(g)}$$

Formulae of Salts

You need to remember the formulae of the salts listed in this table:

Group	Salt	Formula
1	Sodium chloride	$NaCl$
1	Potassium chloride	KCl
1	Sodium carbonate	Na_2CO_3
1	Sodium nitrate	$NaNO_3$
1	Sodium sulfate	Na_2SO_4
2	Magnesium sulfate	$MgSO_4$
2	Magnesium carbonate	$MgCO_3$
2	Magnesium oxide	MgO
2	Magnesium chloride	$MgCl_2$
2	Calcium carbonate	$CaCO_3$
2	Calcium chloride	$CaCl_2$
2	Calcium sulfate	$CaSO_4$

Magnesium Sulfate Solution

HT You should already know how to write formulae for **ionic compounds**. Given the formulae of the salts listed in the table, you need to be able to work out the charge on each ion in a compound.

Energy Changes in Chemical Reactions

Exothermic changes (like combustion) release energy...
- usually as heat
- because the products have less energy than the reactants did.

Endothermic changes...
- are less common than exothermic changes
- take in energy, so usually feel cold to the touch. This means the products have more energy than the reactants did.

Endothermic reactions in industry can take a lot of energy to make them happen. Exothermic reactions can sometimes be dangerous because they can reach very high temperatures if they aren't adequately controlled.

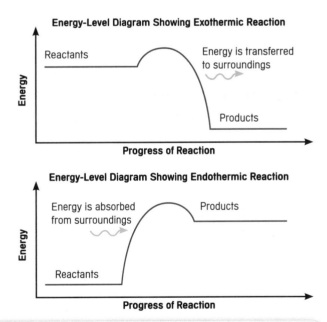

Energy-Level Diagram Showing Exothermic Reaction

Energy

Reactants

Energy is transferred to surroundings

Products

Progress of Reaction

Energy-Level Diagram Showing Endothermic Reaction

Energy

Energy is absorbed from surroundings

Products

Reactants

Progress of Reaction

Quick Test

1. Describe the hazard symbols for toxic and flammable.
2. State the formulae of hydrochloric acid and sulfuric acid.
3. What is the formula of sodium hydroxide?
4. HT Write a balanced symbol equation to show the reaction of magnesium oxide and nitric acid.

C6 Chemical Synthesis

Percentage Yield

When chemical synthesis takes place, the starting materials (**reactants**) react to produce new substances (**products**). The greater the amount of reactants used, the greater the amount of product formed.

You can calculate the **percentage yield** by comparing...
- the actual yield – actual amount of product made
- the theoretical yield – amount of product you would expect to get if the reaction goes to completion.

$$\text{Percentage yield} = \frac{\text{Actual yield}}{\text{Theoretical yield}} \times 100$$

Chemical Synthesis

There are a number of different stages in any chemical synthesis of an inorganic compound:

1 Establish the **reaction** or series of reactions that are needed to make the **product**.

2 Carry out a risk assessment.

(HT) You need to work out the quantities of reactants to use.

3 Carry out the reaction under suitable conditions, e.g. temperature, concentration and use of a **catalyst**.

4 Separate the product from the reaction mixture.

5 **Purify** the product to ensure it's not contaminated by other products or **reactants**.

6 Weigh the mass and calculate the **percentage yield**.

7 Check the **yield** and **purity** by **titration**.

N.B. The purity of a product is important as impurities can be dangerous.

Ways of Purifying a Product

1. Filtration separates insoluble solids from dissolved substances.

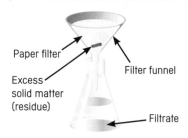

Paper filter
Filter funnel
Excess solid matter (residue)
Filtrate

2. Heating evaporates away the solvent (water) to leave behind crystals of the product. You can also make crystals by cooling the mixture.

Heat

3. Drying the product in a desiccator.

Checking the Purity

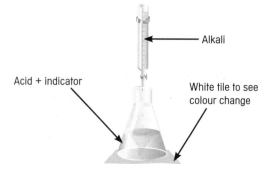

Alkali
Acid + indicator
White tile to see colour change

Relative Atomic Mass

The **relative atomic mass** (RAM) of an **element** shows the mass of one **atom** in comparison to the mass of other atoms.

You can obtain the relative atomic mass of an element by looking at the periodic table.

Examples are…

- RAM of Mg = 24
- RAM of Cu = 63.5
- RAM of C = 12
- RAM of K = 39.

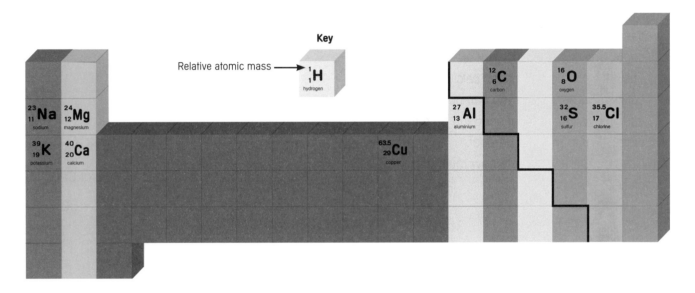

Relative Formula Mass

The **relative formula mass** (RFM or M_r) of a compound is the relative atomic masses of all its elements added together.

To calculate the RFM you need to know…
- the formula of the compound
- the RAM of each of the atoms involved.

Example

Calculate the RFM of water, H_2O.

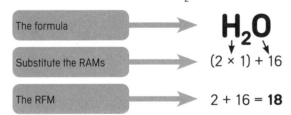

The formula → H_2O

Substitute the RAMs → $(2 \times 1) + 16$

The RFM → $2 + 16 = \mathbf{18}$

HT Quantity of Reactants

In chemical synthesis you need to work out how much of each reactant is required to make a known amount of product. To do this you need to know…
- how to find its relative atomic mass from the periodic table
- how to calculate its relative formula mass

- that a balanced equation shows the number of atoms or molecules of the reactants and products taking part in the reaction
- how to work out the ratio of the mass of reactants to the mass of products
- how to apply the ratio to the question.

C6 Chemical Synthesis

HT Finding the Mass of a Product

Example

Calculate how much calcium oxide can be produced from 50kg of calcium carbonate. (Relative atomic masses: Ca = 40, C = 12, O = 16).

1 Write down the equation.

2 Work out the RFM of each substance.

3 Check that the total mass of reactants equals the total mass of the products. If they aren't the same, check your work.

4 The question only mentions calcium oxide and calcium carbonate, so you can now ignore the carbon dioxide. You just need the ratio of mass of reactant to mass of product.

5 Use the ratio to calculate how much calcium oxide can be produced.

1
$$CaCO_3 \rightarrow CaO + CO_2$$

2
$$40 + 12 + (3 \times 16) \rightarrow (40 + 16) + [12 + (2 \times 16)]$$

3
$$100 \rightarrow 56 + 44 \checkmark$$

4
$$100 : 56$$

5
If 100kg of $CaCO_3$ produces 56kg of CaO,

then 1kg of $CaCO_3$ produces $\frac{56}{100}$ kg of CaO,

and 50kg of $CaCO_3$ produces $\frac{56}{100} \times 50$

= 28kg of CaO

Finding the Mass of a Reactant

Example

Calculate how much aluminium oxide is needed to produce 540 tonnes of aluminium. (Relative atomic masses: Al = 27, O = 16).

1 Write down the equation.

2 Work out the RFM of each substance.

3 Check that the total mass of reactants equals the total mass of the products. If they aren't the same, check your work.

4 The question only mentions aluminium oxide and aluminium, so you can now ignore the oxygen. You just need the ratio of mass of reactant to mass of product.

5 Use the ratio to calculate how much aluminium oxide is needed.

1
$$2Al_2O_3 \rightarrow 4Al + 3O_2$$

2
$$2[(2 \times 27) + (3 \times 16)] \rightarrow (4 \times 27) + [3 \times (2 \times 16)]$$

3
$$204 \rightarrow 108 + 96 \checkmark$$

4
$$204 : 108$$

5
If 204 tonnes of Al_2O_3 produces 108 tonnes of Al,

then $\frac{204}{108}$ tonnes is needed to produce 1 tonne of Al,

and $\frac{204}{108} \times 540$ tonnes is needed to

produce 540 tonnes of Al

= 1020 tonnes of Al_2O_3

Titration

Titration can be used to calculate the concentration of an **acid** by finding out how much **alkali** is needed to **neutralise** it.

Use this method:

1 Fill a burette with an alkali (of known concentration) and take an initial reading of the volume.

2 If you have been given a solid acid, accurately weigh out a sample of it and dissolve it in an accurately measured volume of distilled water.

3 Use a pipette to measure the aqueous acid into a conical flask. By using a pipette you will know the precise amount of acid used.

4 Now add a few drops of the indicator phenolphthalein (it should stay colourless).

5 Add alkali from the burette to the acid in the flask drop by drop.

6 Swirl the flask to mix it well. Near the end of the reaction, the indicator will start to turn pink. When the colour changes permanently, it means that the acid has been neutralised.

7 Record the volume of alkali added by subtracting the initial burette reading from the final burette reading.

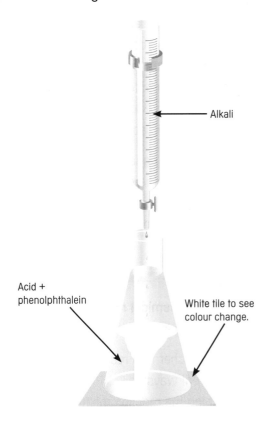

Alkali

Acid + phenolphthalein

White tile to see colour change.

Collecting Titration Data

In order to make sure that your titration result is a good estimate of the true value being measured, you'll need to repeat the titration. If one of the results is very different from the majority of the results, it could indicate that an error was made. This result should be repeated and perhaps ignored. Usually, when performing a titration, you repeat the experiment until you get two results that are the same.

Quick Test

1 What is the RFM of $MgCO_3$?

2 If the theoretical yield is 80kg but the actual yield is 60kg, what is the percentage yield?

3 Suggest three ways to purify a product.

4 How could you measure the yield and purity of a product?

5 HT What mass of CO_2 will be produced when 200kg of $CaCO_3$ is heated?
The equation is $CaCO_3 \longrightarrow CaO + CO_2$

C6 Chemical Synthesis

Interpreting Titration Results

You may be asked to use a given formula to analyse some titration results.

Example

1.5g of impure citric acid was dissolved into 50cm³ of water, and then sodium hydroxide (NaOH) was added from a burette until the acid was neutralised. The concentration of the sodium hydroxide solution was 20g/dm³ and 34.4cm³ was required to neutralise the citric acid in the conical flask.

Use the following equation to calculate the mass of pure citric acid in the sample. Use your answer to calculate the purity of the acid, as a percentage, using the equation provided.

$$\text{Mass of pure citric acid} = \frac{192 \times \text{Volume of NaOH} \times \text{Concentration of NaOH}}{120\,000}$$

So...

$$\text{Mass of pure citric acid} = \frac{192 \times 34.4 \times 20}{120\,000}$$
$$= \mathbf{1.10g}$$

$$\text{Percentage purity} = \frac{\text{Actual mass of pure substance}}{\text{Mass of impure substance}} \times 100$$

So...

$$\text{Percentage purity} = \frac{1.10}{1.50} \times 100$$
$$= \mathbf{73\%}$$

Rates of Reactions

The rate of a **chemical reaction** is the amount of products made in a given unit of time.

The rate of a chemical reaction can be found in three different ways:
1. Weighing the reaction mixture.
2. Measuring the volume of gas produced.
3. Observing the formation of a precipitate.

Weighing the reaction mixture – If one of the products is a gas, you could weigh the reaction mixture at timed intervals. The mass of the mixture will decrease as the gas is produced.

Measuring the volume of gas produced – You could use a gas syringe to measure the total volume of gas produced at timed intervals.

Observing the formation of a precipitate – This can be done by...
- watching a cross on a tile underneath the jar to see when it's no longer visible
- monitoring a colour change using a light sensor.

Weighing the Reaction Mixture

Measuring the Volume of Gas Produced

Observing the Formation of a Precipitate

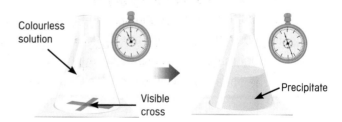

Colourless solution

Visible cross

Precipitate

Changing the Rate of Reaction

There are four important factors that speed up the rate of reaction:

1 Increasing the **temperature**.

2 Increasing the **concentration** of dissolved reactants.

3 Increasing the **surface area** by grinding lumps into powders.

4 Using a **catalyst**.

Collision Theory

It's easy to do experiments that show a correlation between increasing the concentration of a dissolved reactant and the rate of reaction.

However, a plausible scientific explanation of the link must also be found before the relationship can be considered to be an example of cause and effect.

Collision theory states that for two reactant particles to react, they must collide. But when they collide, they need to have enough energy so that they don't simply bounce off each other. This is called the **activation energy**.

If the reactant particles collide more **frequently**, the reaction will speed up. If the particles collide with more energy, they're more likely to have successful collisions, which will also speed up the reaction.

Concentration of Dissolved Reactants

In a **low concentration** reaction, there are fewer particles of **reactant** and the particles are more spread out. This means that the particles will collide less frequently.

In a **high concentration** reaction, there are more particles of reactant and the particles are crowded close together. This means that the particles will collide more frequently.

Low Concentration

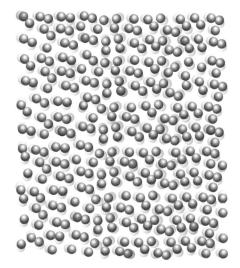

High Concentration

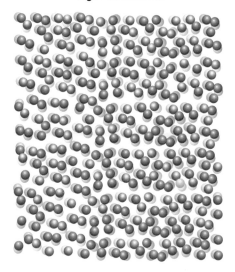

Key Water ● Reactant

C6 Chemical Synthesis

Surface Area of Solid Reactants

Large particles (for example, lumps of solid) have a **small surface area** in relation to their volume, which means that…

- fewer particles are exposed and available for collisions
- collisions are less frequent, so the reaction is slower.

Small particles (for example, powdered solids) have a **large surface area** in relation to their volume, which means that…

- more particles are exposed and available for collisions
- collisions are more frequent, so the reaction is faster.

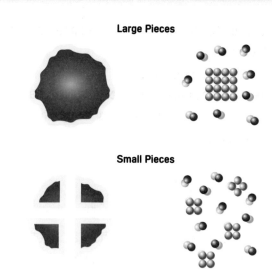

Large Pieces

Small Pieces

Using a Catalyst

Catalysts increase the rate of chemical reactions without being used up or changed during the process.

A catalyst…

- lowers the amount of energy needed for a successful collision
- makes more of the collisions successful
- speeds up the reaction.

Different reactions need different catalysts, for example…

- the production of ammonia uses an iron catalyst
- the production of sulfuric acid uses vanadium(V) oxide catalyst
- the production of nitric acid uses platinum / rhodium gauze catalyst.

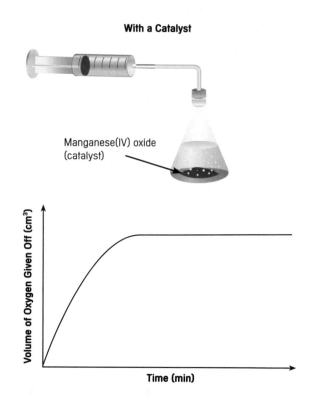

Without a Catalyst

Gas syringe measures volume of oxygen given off

Hydrogen peroxide

With a Catalyst

Manganese(IV) oxide (catalyst)

Analysing the Rate of Reaction

Graphs can be plotted to show the progress of a chemical reaction. There are three things you need to remember:

- The steeper the line, the faster the reaction.
- When one of the **reactants** is used up the reaction stops (line becomes flat).
- The same amount of **product** is formed from the same amount of **reactants**, irrespective of rate.

The graph shows that reaction A is faster than reaction B. This could be because…

- the surface area of the solid reactants in reaction A is greater than in reaction B
- the temperature of reaction A is greater than reaction B
- the concentration of the solution in reaction A is greater than in reaction B
- a catalyst is used in reaction A but not in reaction B.

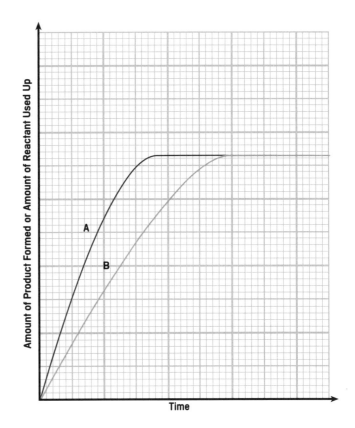

Controlling a Chemical Reaction

When carrying out a chemical synthesis on an industrial scale there are economic and safety factors to consider.

Examples of economic factors are as follows:

- The rate of manufacture must be high enough to produce a sufficient daily **yield** of product.
- Percentage yield must be high enough to produce a sufficient daily yield of product.
- A low percentage yield is acceptable providing the reaction can be repeated many times with recycled starting materials.
- Optimum conditions should be used that give the lowest cost rather than the fastest reaction or highest percentage yield.

Examples of safety factors are as follows:

- Care must be taken when using any reactants or products that could harm the environment if there was a leak.

- Care must be taken to avoid putting any harmful by-products into the environment.
- A risk assessment must be carried out, and the necessary precautions taken.

Quick Test

1. Define the term 'rate of reaction'.
2. List three ways to measure the rate of a reaction.
3. Why would chemists want to speed up the rate of an industrial reaction?
4. Explain why increasing the concentration speeds up a reaction.
5. Explain why powders react faster than lumps.
6. State three key points about a catalyst.

C6 Exam Practice Questions

1 Sherbet can be made by mixing three ingredients: sugar, citric acid and sodium hydrogencarbonate. When you put the sherbet in your mouth, the ingredients dissolve in your saliva and a neutralisation reaction occurs that produces a gas.

(a) What would you expect the pH of a solution of citric acid to be? **[1]**

....

(b) Complete the word equation for the reaction that occurs when sherbet dissolves in saliva. **[3]**

.... + Sodium hydrogencarbonate ➡ Sodium citrate + ... + ...

(c) Sometimes people suffer from acid indigestion, in which they have too much hydrochloric acid in their stomach. Martin suggests that this could be neutralised by swallowing tablets that contain magnesium, because he knows that magnesium reacts with acids to produce a neutral salt.

(i) Write a word equation for the reaction between magnesium and hydrochloric acid. **[2]**

....

(ii) Why is Martin's suggestion dangerous? **[1]**

....

(iii) It's safer to treat acid indigestion using tablets that contain calcium carbonate or magnesium carbonate. Suggest why, using word equations to help explain your answer. **[3]**

....

....

....

....

2 Pam works for a company that manufactures fertilisers.

(a) One of the fertilisers that she makes is ammonium nitrate. It's made from ammonium hydroxide (an alkali) and nitric acid.

(i) Which ion is present in all acids? **[1]**

....

(ii) Which ion is present in all alkalis? **[1]**

....

(iii) Write an ionic equation, including state symbols, for the reaction between these two ions in a neutralisation reaction. **[2]**

....

....

(b) Pam makes a small quantity of ammonium nitrate, using a titration. Here are some of the steps that she follows. Fill in the empty boxes to put the steps in the correct order. Three have been done for you. **[3]**

A   Place some ammonium hydroxide into a conical flask and some nitric acid into a burette.

B   Heat the solution to evaporate some of the water.

C   Add two drops of indicator to the conical flask.

D   Allow the solution to cool and crystals of ammonium nitrate to form.

E   Add the nitric acid from the burette into the conical flask until the indicator changes colour.

F   Dry the product in an oven or desiccator.

G   Repeat the titration using the correct volume of acid and alkali but with no indicator.

A				F	G

HT **3** Gill investigates the reaction between magnesium carbonate and nitric acid, which produces magnesium nitrate, carbon dioxide and water. Here is a balanced symbol equation for this reaction:

$$MgCO_3 + 2HNO_3 \longrightarrow Mg(NO_3)_2 + H_2O + CO_2$$

Gill measures the rate of the reaction by measuring the amount of gas given off every 10 seconds. Here is a graph of her results:

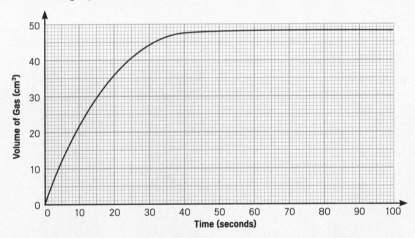

(a) What volume of gas was given off after 10 seconds? **[1]**

(b) Suggest two ways that Gill could increase the rate of the reaction. **[2]**

(c) Gill starts the reaction with 8.4g of magnesium carbonate. What mass of magnesium nitrate should she expect to produce? **[3]**

Velocity

Velocity tells you an object's…
- speed
- direction of travel.

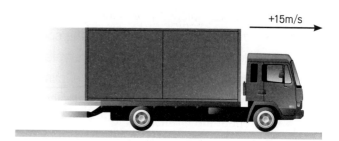

+15m/s

HT For example, if a lorry travels along a straight road at 15m/s (metres per second), in one direction, the velocity is +15m/s. If it then travels in the opposite direction at the same speed, the velocity is -15m/s.

It doesn't matter which direction is called **positive** or **negative** as long as opposite directions have opposite signs.

-15m/s

This idea is also used when describing **distance**:
- Changes in distance in one direction are described as positive.
- In the opposite direction they're negative.

Calculating Speed

To calculate an object's speed you need to know…
- the **distance** it has travelled
- the **time** it took to travel that distance.

You can calculate speed using this formula:

$$\text{Speed (m/s)} = \frac{\text{Distance travelled (m)}}{\text{Time taken (s)}}$$

$$\frac{d}{s \times t}$$

The formula calculates an **average speed** over the total distance travelled, even if the speed of an object isn't constant.

The speed of an object at a particular point in time is called the **instantaneous speed**.

Example

A car travels 10 metres in five seconds. What is its average speed?

$$\text{Speed} = \frac{\text{Distance travelled}}{\text{Time taken}} = \frac{10\text{m}}{5\text{s}} = \textbf{2m/s}$$

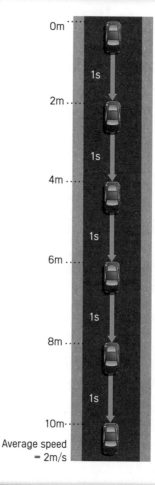

0m
1s
2m
1s
4m
1s
6m
1s
8m
1s
10m
Average speed = 2m/s

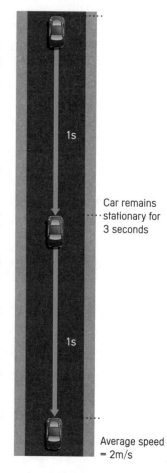

1s

Car remains stationary for 3 seconds

1s

Average speed = 2m/s

Distance–Time Graphs

The slope, or **gradient**, of a **distance–time graph** is a measure of the **speed** of the object. The **steeper the slope**, the **greater the speed**.

The graph shows the following:

1. A stationary person standing 15m away from point O.
2. A person moving at a constant speed.
3. A person moving at a greater constant speed.

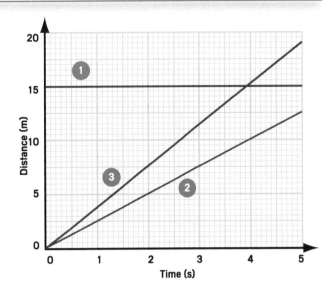

HT Displacement–Time Graphs

You can calculate the speed of an object by working out the gradient of a displacement–time graph:

1. Take any two points on the gradient.
2. Read off the displacement travelled between these points.
3. Note the time taken between these points.
4. Divide the displacement by the time.

For example:

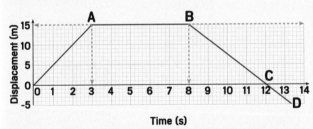

Speed from O to A = $\dfrac{15m}{3s}$ = **5m/s**

Speed from A to B = $\dfrac{15m - 15m}{5s}$ = **0m/s**

Speed from B to C = $\dfrac{15m}{4s}$ = **3.75m/s**

Speed from C to D = **3.75m/s**

So, the object…

- travelled at 5m/s for three seconds
- remained stationary for five seconds
- travelled at 3.75m/s for four seconds back to the starting point
- continued with a negative speed to point D. The displacement is now negative.

Remember…

- this calculation only works when looking at straight line sections
- when the object reaches point C, the average velocity for the journey is O because it's back where it started
- if you're asked to give velocity you need to indicate the direction. If the velocity in the first section is positive, the velocity in the last section will be negative because the object is moving in the opposite direction
- the displacement of an object at a given moment is its net distance from its starting point together with an indication of direction. So, the displacement at C is O
- the gradient of a displacement–time graph is the velocity (the velocity is negative between points B and D because the gradient is negative).

P4 Explaining Motion

Curvy Distance–Time Graphs

The **instantaneous velocity** of an object is its instantaneous speed together with an indication of direction.

HT When the line of a **distance–time graph** is curved, it means the **speed** of an object is **changing**:

- O to A – the line is curved. The object must be speeding up because the gradient is increasing.
- A to B – the line curves the other way. The object must be slowing down because the gradient is decreasing.

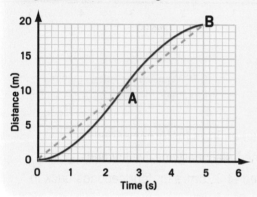

Because the graph is curved it's difficult to work out the **instantaneous speed**, but you can work out the average speed by dividing the total distance by the total time.

$$\text{Speed} = \frac{\text{Distance}}{\text{Time}}$$

$$= \frac{20m}{5s}$$

$$= \textbf{4m/s}$$

The dashed line shows the average speed. Where the gradient is...

- **steeper** than the dashed line, the object is travelling **faster** than the average speed
- **less steep** than the dashed line, the object is travelling **slower** than the average speed.

Speed–Time Graphs

The slope, or **gradient**, of a **speed–time graph** represents how quickly an object is increasing in speed (i.e. **accelerating**). The steeper the slope, the faster its speed is increasing.

Speed–time graphs are used in **lorry tachographs** to make sure that drivers...

- don't exceed the speed limit
- rest for suitable amounts of time.

Object is stationary.

Object is moving at a constant speed.

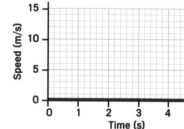

Object is accelerating.

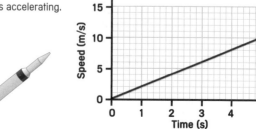

Quick Test

1. A student plots a speed–time graph. The graph gives a horizontal straight line. What does that tell you about the acceleration?
2. HT A man walks North at 2m/s for 10 seconds, then rests for another 20s. What is his displacement?

HT Understanding Velocity–Time Graphs

The quantity **velocity** has both **speed** and **direction**. A change in either (or both) the speed or direction of travel will cause a change in velocity. A velocity–time graph can have negative values for the velocity axis.

Look at the first velocity–time graph shown opposite:
- Car A is at rest.
- Car B is travelling with a constant velocity of 18m/s.
- Car C has a constantly increasing velocity (accelerating).
- Car D has a velocity that is decreasing at a constant rate (decelerating).

The second velocity–time graph shows a ball travelling at a constant speed of 10m/s, in one direction, for two seconds. It has an elastic collision with a wall before rebounding in the opposite direction at the same speed. Notice that the velocity will have changed because the direction of travel has changed. The speed remains constant at 10m/s.

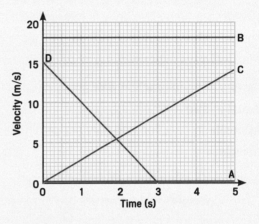

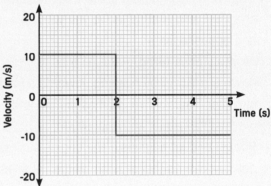

Calculating Acceleration

Acceleration, change in speed and time are related by this formula:

$$\text{Acceleration (m/s}^2) = \frac{\text{Change in speed (m/s)}}{\text{Time taken (s)}}$$

where v is change in speed, a is acceleration and t is time taken

$$\frac{v}{a \times t}$$

Example
A car is travelling at 2m/s when the driver accelerates to 10m/s in four seconds. What is the acceleration?

$$\text{Acceleration} = \frac{\text{Change in speed}}{\text{Time taken}}$$

$$\text{Acceleration} = \frac{10 - 2}{4}$$

$$= \frac{8}{4}$$

$$= 2\text{m/s}^2$$

HT Example
The graph shows the motion of a car accelerating from rest. Use the graph to calculate the car's acceleration.

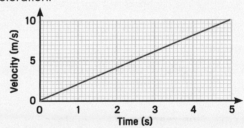

The gradient of a velocity–time graph can be used to find the acceleration.

$$\text{Gradient (acceleration, m/s}^2) = \frac{\text{Change in velocity (m/s)}}{\text{Time taken (s)}}$$

$$= \frac{10 - 0\text{m/s}}{5\text{s}}$$

$$= 2\text{m/s}^2$$

Forces

A **force** occurs when two objects **interact** with each other. Whenever one object exerts a force on another, it always experiences a force in return.

The forces in an **interaction pair** are...
- **equal** in size
- **opposite** in direction and they act on different objects.

Here are some examples of forces in action:
- **Gravity (weight)** – two masses are attracted to each other, e.g. you are attracted to the Earth and the Earth is attracted to you with an equal and opposite force.
- **Air resistance (drag)** – the air tries to slow down a skydiver by pushing upwards against him / her. The skydiver pushes the air out of the way with an equal and opposite force.
- **Rocket and jet engines** – the engine pushes gas backwards (action) and the gas pushes the rocket forwards (reaction).

HT A person moves by applying a force to the ground (they push on the ground). There will be an equal and opposite force generated (the ground pushes back on the person). The person moves because they have a much smaller mass than the Earth.

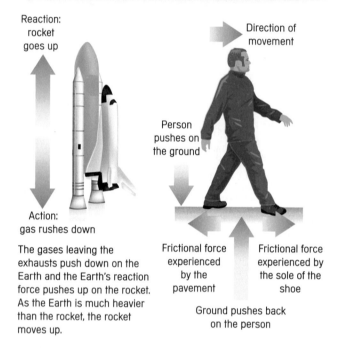

Reaction: rocket goes up

Action: gas rushes down

The gases leaving the exhausts push down on the Earth and the Earth's reaction force pushes up on the rocket. As the Earth is much heavier than the rocket, the rocket moves up.

Direction of movement

Person pushes on the ground

Frictional force experienced by the pavement

Frictional force experienced by the sole of the shoe

Ground pushes back on the person

Friction and Reaction

Some forces only occur as a response to another force.

When an object is resting on a surface...
- the object is pulled down onto the surface by gravity
- the surface pushes up on the object with an equal force.

This is called the **reaction of the surface**.

When two objects try to slide past one another, both objects experience a force that tries to **stop them moving**. This is called **friction**.

Objects don't have to be moving to experience friction. For example, the friction from a car's brakes stops it rolling down a hill.

Friction and the reaction of a surface arise in response to the action of an applied force, and their size matches the applied force up to a limit.

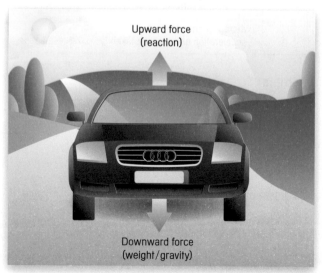

Upward force (reaction)

Downward force (weight / gravity)

Forces and Motion

Arrows are used when drawing diagrams of **forces**:

- The size of the arrow represents the size of the force.
- The direction of the arrow shows the direction the force is acting in.

N.B. Force arrows are always drawn with the tail of the arrow touching the object even if the force is pushing the object.

If more than one force acts on an object they will...
- add up if they are acting in the same direction
- subtract if they are acting in opposite directions.

The overall effect of adding or subtracting these forces is called the **resultant force**.

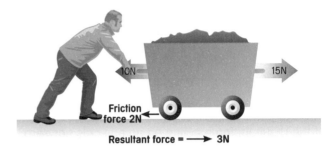

Momentum

Momentum is a measure of the motion of an object.

You can calculate the momentum of an object using this formula:

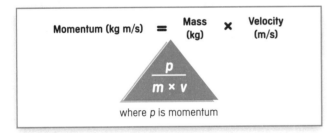

where *p* is momentum

If a car and a lorry are travelling at the same speed, the lorry will have more momentum because it has a bigger mass.

Example

A car has a mass of 1200kg and is travelling at a velocity of 30m/s. What is its momentum?

Momentum = Mass × Velocity
= 1200kg × 30m/s
= **36 000kg m/s**

P4 Explaining Motion

Change in Momentum

If the **resultant force** acting on an object is **zero**, its momentum will **not change**. So, if the object is…

- stationary, it will remain stationary
- already moving, it will continue moving in a straight line at a steady speed.

If the resultant force acting on an object is **not zero**, it causes a **change** of momentum in the direction of the force. This could…

- make a stationary object move
- increase or decrease an object's speed
- change an object's direction.

The extent of the change in momentum depends on…

- the size of the resultant force
- the length of time the force is acting on the object.

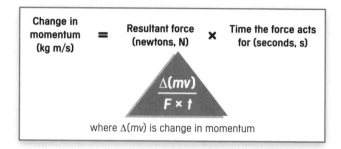

| Change in momentum (kg m/s) | = | Resultant force (newtons, N) | × | Time the force acts for (seconds, s) |

$$\frac{\Delta(mv)}{F \times t}$$

where $\Delta(mv)$ is change in momentum

Collisions

Collisions can cause changes in an object's momentum. For example, a car with a mass of 1000kg, travelling at 10m/s, has a momentum of 10 000kg m/s. If the car is involved in a collision and comes to a sudden stop, it would experience a change in momentum of 10 000kg m/s.

Sudden changes in momentum as a result of a collision can affect…

- the car
- the passengers – leading to injuries.

If the change in momentum is **spread** out over a longer period of time, the resultant force will be **smaller**.

Safety Devices

The force of the **impact** on the human body can be reduced by increasing the **time** of the impact. This is the purpose of road safety devices, for example…

- seat belts
- crumple zones – crumple on impact (e.g. motorcycle and bicycle helmets)
- air bags.

Crumple zone

Speeding Up and Slowing Down

Cars and bicycles have a...

- **driving force** produced by the engine (car) or the energy of the cyclist (bicycle)
- **counter force** caused by **friction** and air resistance.

If the driving force is...

- **bigger than** the counter force, the vehicle speeds up
- **equal to** the counter force, the vehicle travels at a constant speed in a straight line
- **smaller than** the counter force, the vehicle slows down.

Car Speeds Up

Counter force 100N ◄——— Car ———► Driving force 500N

Car Travels at a Constant Speed

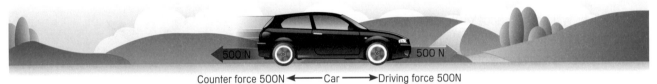

Counter force 500N ◄——— Car ———► Driving force 500N

Car Slows Down

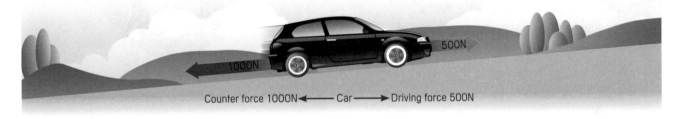

Counter force 1000N ◄——— Car ———► Driving force 500N

Kinetic Energy

A moving object has **kinetic energy**.

The amount of kinetic energy an object has depends on its...

- **mass**
- **velocity**.

The greater the mass and velocity of an object, the more kinetic energy it has. You can calculate kinetic energy using this formula:

$$\text{Kinetic energy (joules, J)} = \frac{1}{2} \times \text{Mass (kilograms, kg)} \times \text{Velocity}^2 \text{ (metres per second, m/s)}^2$$

$$\frac{KE}{\frac{1}{2} \times m \times v^2}$$

Example

A bicycle of mass 50kg is moving at a velocity of 8m/s. How much kinetic energy does it have?

$$\begin{aligned}
\text{Kinetic energy} &= \frac{1}{2} \times \text{Mass} \times \text{Velocity}^2 \\
&= \frac{1}{2} \times 50\text{kg} \times (8\text{m/s})^2 \\
&= \frac{1}{2} \times 50 \times 64 \\
&= \mathbf{1600J}
\end{aligned}$$

P4 Explaining Motion

Objects Thrown Upwards

Consider a person throwing a ball up in the air. As the ball leaves the hand, an initial force is applied vertically upwards. There will be two forces opposing the motion:
- **Air resistance**
- **Gravity**.

As soon as the ball leaves the hand, these forces will cause the ball to lose speed. There is no upward force once the ball has left the hand.

Objects Falling

Consider a skydiver jumping out of a plane. As the skydiver jumps out of the plane, only one force is acting in the vertical direction – the unbalanced force of **gravity**.

The skydiver will start to accelerate downwards:

1. As the skydiver falls, he / she will start to experience a new force of **air resistance**. The faster the skydiver falls, the greater this air resistance force becomes.
2. The force of gravity remains the same.
3. Eventually the two forces of gravity and air resistance become equal and opposite.
4. The skydiver now stops accelerating and travels at a constant speed.

Work and Energy

Work is done by a force to move an object, resulting in the **transfer** of **energy**.

When work is done…
- **on** an object, the object **gains** energy
- **by** an object, the object **loses** energy.

The total amount of energy remains the same, i.e. energy is **conserved**.

Amount of energy transferred (joules, J) = Work done (joules, J)

When a force makes an object's velocity increase…
- work is done on the object by the force
- the object gains kinetic energy.

If you ignore drag and friction, the increase in kinetic energy will be **equal to** the work done by the force. But, in reality, some of the energy will be dissipated (lost) as heat.

The relationship between work done, force and distance is shown by this formula:

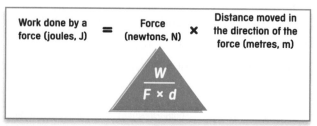

| Work done by a force (joules, J) | = | Force (newtons, N) | × | Distance moved in the direction of the force (metres, m) |

$$\frac{W}{F \times d}$$

Air resistance or friction will cause the gain in an object's kinetic energy to be less than the work done on it by an applied force in the direction of motion because some energy is dissipated through heating.

Gravitational Potential Energy

When an object is lifted above the ground…

- work is done by the lifting force against gravity
- the object has the potential to do work when it falls, e.g. a diver standing on a diving board.

This is called **gravitational potential energy** (**GPE**).

You can calculate change in GPE using this formula:

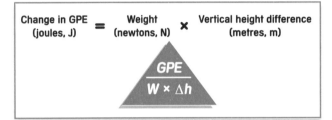

| Change in GPE (joules, J) | = | Weight (newtons, N) | × | Vertical height difference (metres, m) |

$$\frac{GPE}{W \times \Delta h}$$

N.B. To find the GPE, you use weight not mass.

If an object is dropped, its GPE decreases and converts into kinetic energy.

Example

An object is dropped from a height of 5m. It has a mass of 2kg and weighs 20N. How much kinetic energy does it gain?

Change in GPE = Weight × Vertical height difference

= 20N × 5m

= **100J**

The object…

- loses 100J of gravitational potential energy
- gains 100J of kinetic energy.

(HT) You can use the kinetic energy formula to work out the velocity of a falling object. In the example above we know that the object has gained 100J of kinetic energy.

Kinetic energy = $\frac{1}{2}$ × Mass × Velocity²

$100 = \frac{1}{2} \times 2 \times v^2$

$100 = v^2$

$v = \sqrt{100}$

= **10m/s**

Quick Test

1. With a rocket, the engine pushes gas backwards. What is the name of that force?
2. A force of 12N acts on a truck for two seconds. What is the change in momentum?
3. Give three examples of safety devices used in cars.
4. A cyclist of mass 60kg is moving at a speed of 4m/s. How much kinetic energy does the cyclist have?
5. (HT) A person weighing 800N gains 16 000J of gravitational potential energy as they're carried up in a lift. How high did they go?
6. (HT) A person has 800J of kinetic energy. If they have a mass of 100kg, how fast are they travelling?

P4 Exam Practice Questions

1 (a) The graph shows three different journeys. Match statements **A, B** and **C** with the labels **1–3** on the graph.

   A The person is moving at the fastest speed. ⬭

   B The person is moving at the slowest speed. ⬭

   C The person is stationary. ⬭

[2]

(b) What does the gradient of a distance–time graph tell you? **[1]**

....

2 (a) A car is measured travelling 40 metres in 5 seconds. How fast is the car travelling? Put a ⬭ring⬭ around the correct answer. **[1]**

   200m/s   **8m**   **20m/s**   **8m/s**   **200m**

(b) A motorcycle accelerates from rest and reaches a speed of 30m/s in 4 seconds. What is the acceleration of the motorcycle? Put a ⬭ring⬭ around the correct answer. **[1]**

   120m/s²   **7.5m/s**   **120m/s**   **34m/s**   **7.5m/s²**

3 Which of the following statements are correct? Put ticks (✓) in the boxes next to the **two** correct statements. **[2]**

Speed–time graphs are used in lorry tachographs to make sure drivers rest for the appropriate time. ⬭

Friction is a force that always opposes motion. ⬭

The instantaneous speed is the maximum speed reached during a journey. ⬭

The gradient of a distance–time graph is the acceleration. ⬭

4 A person starts to walk in a straight line along a flat pavement. Explain what forces are involved in the process of walking. **[6]**

✏ *The quality of written communication will be assessed in your answer to this question.*

....

....

....

....

....

....

....

5 A car of mass 1500kg is travelling along a road at a velocity of 45m/s.

(a) What is the momentum of the car? **[2]**

(b) What is the acceleration if the speed increases from 45m/s to 55m/s in 4 seconds? **[2]**

6 Which of the following statements are correct? Put ticks (✓) in the boxes next to the **two** correct statements. **[2]**

The change in momentum depends on the size of the force acting and the time it acts for. ☐

For an object moving in a straight line, if the driving force is larger than friction, the object will slow down. ☐

If the resultant force on a car is zero, its momentum is constant. ☐

The energy of a moving object is called work. ☐

HT **7** A ball of weight 40N is dropped from a height of 20 metres. Calculate the velocity of the ball just before it hits the ground. Take the mass of the ball to be 4kg. **[2]**

8 A 150kg dodgem car travelling at 3m/s collides with a rubber wall in the fairground and rebounds with a speed of 2m/s.

(a) What is the change in momentum? **[2]**

(b) If the collision lasted for 0.5 seconds, what force acted on the dodgem car? **[2]**

(c) Why did the driver bend his knees during the impact? **[1]**

P5 Electric Circuits

Static Electricity

When you rub two objects together, they become **electrically charged** as electrons (which are negatively charged) are transferred from one object to the other:

- The object **receiving** the electrons becomes **negatively** charged.
- The object **giving up** electrons becomes **positively** charged.

The electrical charge is called static electricity.

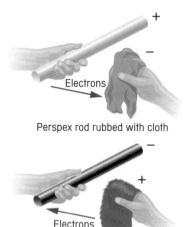

Perspex rod rubbed with cloth

Electrons

Ebonite rod rubbed with fur

Repulsion and Attraction

When two charged materials are brought together, they exert a force on each other:

- Two materials with the same type of charge **repel** each other.
- Two materials with different charges **attract** each other.

For example, if you move...

- a positively charged Perspex rod near to another positively charged Perspex rod suspended on a string, the suspended rod will be **repelled**
- a negatively charged ebonite rod near to a positively charged suspended Perspex rod, the suspended Perspex rod will be **attracted**.

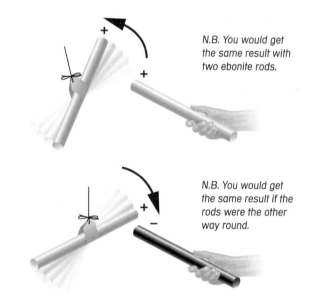

N.B. You would get the same result with two ebonite rods.

N.B. You would get the same result if the rods were the other way round.

Electric Currents

An **electric current** is a **flow of charge**. It's measured in **amperes** (amps).

In an electric circuit...

- the components and wires are full of charges that are free to move
- the battery causes the free charges to move
- the charges aren't used up but flow in a continuous loop.

In **metal conductors** there are lots of charges free to move, but in **insulators** there are no charges free to move.

Metals contain **free electrons** in their structure, which move to create an **electric current**.

Circuit Symbols

Standard symbols are used to represent components in circuits.

Cell	
Power supply (battery)	
Filament lamp	
Switch (open) (closed)	
Light dependent resistor (LDR)	

Fixed resistor	
Variable resistor	
Thermistor	
Voltmeter	
Ammeter	

Types of Current

A **direct current** (d.c.) always flows in the same direction. Cells and batteries supply direct current.

An **alternating current** (a.c.) changes the direction of flow back and forth continuously and is used for mains electricity. The mains supply of **voltage** to your home is 230 volts.

(HT) Alternating current is used for mains supply instead of direct current. This is because...
- it's easier to generate
- it can be distributed more efficiently
- only alternating current can be used in a transformer.

Potential Difference and Current

Potential difference is another name for **voltage**:
- The potential difference between two points in the circuit is the **work done** on (or by) a given amount of charge as it moves between these points.
- It's measured in **volts** (V) using a **voltmeter** connected in parallel across the component.

A bulb with 3 volts across it is taking 3 joules of energy from every unit of charge. This energy is given off as heat and light.

The greater the potential difference across a component, the greater the current will be.

When you add more batteries in series, the potential difference and the current increase.

(HT) When you add more batteries in parallel...
- the total potential difference and current remain the same
- each battery supplies less current.

Increasing the Potential Difference Makes the Bulb Brighter

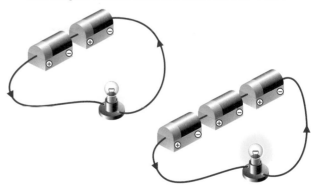

P5 Electric Circuits

Resistance and Current

Components **resist** the flow of **charge** through them. Examples of components are…

* resistors
* lamps
* motors.

The connecting wires in the circuit have some **resistance**, but it's so small that it's usually ignored.

The **greater the resistance** in a circuit, the **smaller the current** will be.

Two lamps together in a circuit with one cell have a certain resistance. If you include another cell in the circuit, it provides…

* a greater **potential difference**
* a greater **current**.

When you add resistors in **series**, the battery has to push charges through more resistors, so the **resistance increases**.

When you add resistors in **parallel**, there are more paths for the charges to flow along, so the total **resistance reduces** and the total **current increases**.

When an electric current flows through a component, it causes the component to heat up. This heating effect is large enough to make a lamp filament glow.

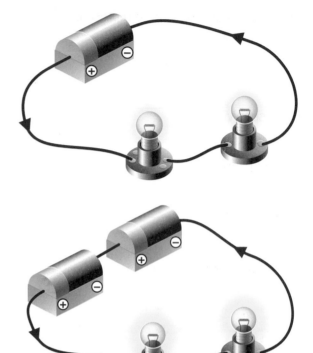

The second circuit has more batteries and so has a higher voltage. This causes a greater current to flow than in the first circuit.

(HT) As the current flows…
* moving charges collide with the vibrating **ions** in the wire, giving them energy
* the increase in energy causes the component to heat up.

Calculating Resistance

You can calculate resistance using this formula:

$$\text{Resistance (ohms, } \Omega) = \frac{\text{Voltage (volts, V)}}{\text{Current (amperes, A)}}$$

$$\frac{V}{I \times R}$$

where *I* is current

Example

A circuit has a current of 3 amps and a voltage of 6V. What is the resistance?

$$\text{Resistance} = \frac{\text{Voltage}}{\text{Current}} = \frac{6V}{3A} = \mathbf{2\Omega}$$

(HT) You can work out the potential difference or current by rearranging the resistance formula.

Example

A circuit has a current of 0.2 amps and a bulb with a resistance of 15 ohms. What is the reading on the voltmeter?

$$\text{Potential difference} = \text{Current} \times \text{Resistance}$$
$$= 0.2A \times 15\Omega$$
$$= \mathbf{3V}$$

Resistance • Current • Potential difference

Current–Voltage Graphs

As long as a component's resistance stays constant, the current through the resistor is **directly proportional** to the **voltage** across the resistor. This is regardless of which direction the current is flowing.

This means that a graph showing current through the component, and voltage across the component, will be a **straight line** through 0.

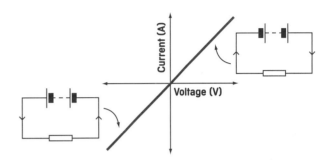

Thermistors and LDRs

The resistance of a **thermistor** depends on its temperature. As the temperature increases…

- its resistance decreases
- more current flows.

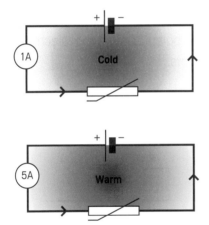

The resistance of a **light dependent resistor (LDR)** depends on light intensity. As the amount of light falling on it increases…

- its resistance decreases
- more current flows.

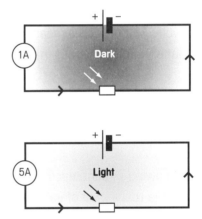

Quick Test

1. If a Perspex rod is rubbed with a cloth, it loses electrons. What charge will the rod now have?
2. What is the circuit symbol for a light dependent resistor?
3. If a battery of 12V is connected across a bulb and a current of 3A flows through it, what is the resistance of the bulb?
4. How could the relationship between the current and voltage across a component be described if the resistance is constant?
5. (HT) A 12V battery is connected across a resistor of resistance 24Ω. What current flows?
6. (HT) Why does a component heat up when a current flows?

P5 Electric Circuits

Series Circuits

When two components are connected in series to a battery…

- the **current** flowing through each component is the same, i.e. $A_1 = A_2 = A_3$
- the **potential difference** across the components adds up to the potential difference across the battery, i.e. $V_1 = V_2 + V_3$
- the potential difference is largest across components with the greatest **resistance**.

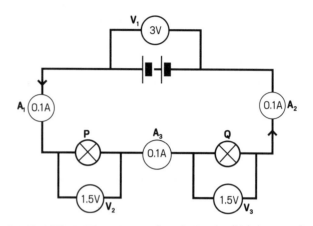

HT The above also applies when **more than two** components are connected in series to a battery.

As shown above right, the voltmeter should be connected in parallel across a component to measure the potential difference between any two chosen points. The voltage across the battery (measured in volts, V) provides a measure of the 'push' of the battery on the charges in the circuit.

HT The work done on each unit of charge by the battery must equal the work done by it on the circuit components. More work is done by the charge moving through a large resistance than through a small one.

A change in the resistance of one component (variable resistor, LDR or thermistor) will result in a change in the potential differences across all the components.

Parallel Circuits

In parallel circuits with one component per parallel path…

- the **current** flowing through each component depends on the **resistance** of each component
- the total current running from (and back to) the battery is equal to the sum of the current through each of the parallel components, i.e. $A_1 = A_2 + A_3 = A_4$
- the current is greatest through the component with the smallest resistance.

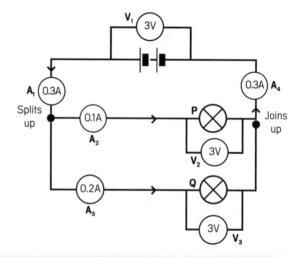

HT The current through each component is the same as if it were the only component present. If a second identical component is added in parallel…

- the same current flows through each component
- the total current through the battery increases.

The same **voltage** causes more current to flow through a smaller resistance than a bigger one.

The **potential difference** across each component is equal to the potential difference of the battery.

Current • Resistance

Electromagnetic Induction

When you move a magnet into a coil of wire, a **voltage** is induced between the ends of the wire because the **magnetic field** is being cut.

If the ends of the coil are connected to make a complete circuit, a **current** will be induced.

This is called **electromagnetic induction**.

Moving the magnet into the coil induces a current in one direction. You can then induce a current in the opposite direction by...
- moving the magnet out of the coil
- moving the other pole of the magnet into the coil.

If there's no movement of the coil or magnet, there's no induced current.

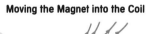
Moving the Magnet into the Coil

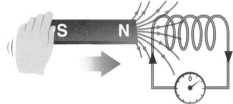

Moving the Magnet out of the Coil

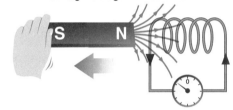

Moving the Other Pole of the Magnet into the Coil

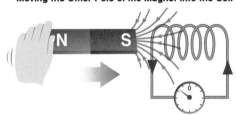

The Electric Generator

Mains electricity is produced by **generators**. Generators use the principle of **electromagnetic induction** to generate electricity by rotating a magnet inside a coil.

The size of the induced voltage can be increased by...
- increasing the speed of rotation of the magnet
- increasing the strength of the magnetic field, possibly by using an electromagnet
- increasing the number of turns on the coil
- placing an iron core inside the coil.

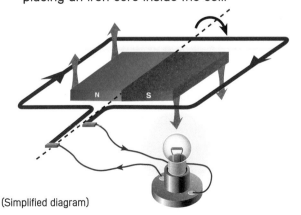

(Simplified diagram)

HT As the magnet rotates, the **voltage** induced in the coil changes direction and size as shown in the diagram. The **current** that's produced is an **alternating current** as it reverses its direction of flow every half turn of the magnet. The direction of the voltage and current after one full turn of the magnet are in the same direction as they were at the start before the magnet was turned.

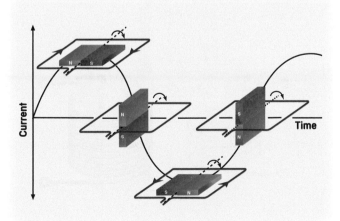

P5 Electric Circuits

Power

When electric charge flows through a component (or device), work is done by the power supply. **Energy is transferred** from the power supply to the component and/or its surroundings.

Power...
- is a measure of the rate of energy transfer to an appliance or device and/or its surroundings
- is measured in watts (W).

You can calculate power using the following formula:

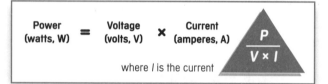

Power (watts, W) = Voltage (volts, V) × Current (amperes, A)

$$\frac{P}{V \times I}$$

where I is the current

Example
An electric motor works at a current of 3A and a voltage of 24V. What is the power of the motor?

Power = Voltage × Current
= 24V × 3A
= **72W**

> **HT** You can work out the potential difference or current by rearranging the power formula.

Example
A 4W light bulb works at a current of 2A. What is the potential difference?

$$\text{Potential difference} = \frac{\text{Power}}{\text{Current}} = \frac{4W}{2A} = \textbf{2V}$$

Transformers

Transformers are used to change the **voltage** of an **alternating current**. They consist of two coils of wire, called the primary and secondary coils, wrapped around a soft iron core.

When two coils of wire are close to each other, a changing magnetic field in one coil caused by changes in the current can induce a voltage in the other:
- Alternating current flowing through the primary coil creates an alternating magnetic field.
- This changing field then induces an alternating current in the secondary coil.

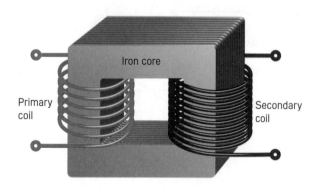

Primary coil

Iron core

Secondary coil

> **HT** The amount by which a transformer changes the voltage depends on the number of turns on the primary and secondary coils. The changing current in the primary coil will cause a changing magnetic field in the iron core, which in turn will cause a changing potential difference across the secondary coil. You need to be able to use this equation:

Voltage on primary coil (V_p) / Voltage on secondary coil (V_s)	=	Number of turns on primary coil, N_p / Number of turns on secondary coil, N_s

Example
A transformer has 1000 turns on the primary coil and 200 turns on the secondary coil. If a voltage of 250V is applied to the primary coil, what is the voltage across the secondary coil?

$$\frac{250}{V_s} = \frac{1000}{200}$$

$$250 = 5V_s \text{ so } V_s = \frac{250}{5} = \textbf{50V}$$

Electric Motors

An electric motor consists of a coil of wire that rotates in between the opposite poles of a permanent magnet, when a current flows through the coil.

A current-carrying wire (or coil)...

- can exert a force on a permanent magnet or another current-carrying wire nearby
- **experiences a force** if placed in a **magnetic field** whose lines of force are at right angles to the wire. The force will be at right angles to **both** the current direction and the lines of force of the **magnetic field**. If the current in a wire travels parallel to the magnetic **field lines**, it doesn't experience a force.

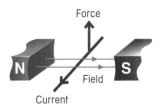

When a current flows through the coil, it will cut the field lines in opposite directions on each side of the coil. This creates a pair of forces in opposite directions and causes the coil to rotate around its axis.

A **commutator** is a rotary switch that turns with the coil, but the brushes that touch it remain fixed. This has the effect of making sure that, as the coil rotates, the current direction into the coil is switched.

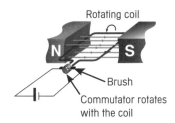

The current always cuts the **field lines** nearest the South pole of the fixed magnet in the same direction, no matter how many times the coil spins.

Similarly, the current will always cut the field lines nearest the North pole in the opposite direction. This produces a pair of opposing forces whose directions remain the same, giving continuous rotation.

Uses of Electric Motors

Electric motors have a role and use in many devices:

Device	How the Motor is Used
Hard disk drive	To rotate the hard disk at high speed under the read / write heads.
DVD player	To rotate the disk so that the information can be read.
Electric motor vehicle	To provide traction via the transmission to the rear wheels.
Washing machine	To rotate the drum and agitate the wash so that all the clothes are washed effectively.
Tumble dryer	To rotate the drum and provide uniform heat to all the items being dried.
Microwave oven	To rotate the food and make sure that it's evenly heated.

Quick Test

1. What principle do generators use to generate electricity?
2. What is the power of a 12V lamp in a circuit where a 0.5A current flows?
3. In a transformer, what induces a voltage across the secondary coil?
4. HT A transformer has a primary coil of 200 turns. If the transformer changes 12V to 240V, how many turns must be on the secondary coil?
5. HT A 60W light bulb has a 240V power supply connected across it. What current flows?

P5 Exam Practice Questions

1. Toni has suspended a positively charged Perspex rod on an insulated plastic thread. What will happen if she brings a negatively charged ebonite rod close to the Perspex rod? **[1]**

....

2. Put a (ring) around the correct symbol for a cell. **[1]**

3. Here is a table of data from an electrical experiment to find the resistance of three components. Complete the table by filling in the missing values.

Component	Voltage (V)	Current (A)	Resistance (Ω)
Lamp	8	....	4
Resistor	....	6	5
Coil	24	4	....

[3]

4. Give two ways to increase the size of an induced voltage in a generator. **[2]**

1. ....

2. ....

5. Chevelle was experimenting by moving a magnet into a coil of wire that was connected to an ammeter. She noticed that the ammeter showed a current flowing in one direction. Four students are discussing how she could reverse the direction of the current.

Jessie
I would move the magnet into the coil more quickly.

Sonny
Try using a coil with more turns on it.

Jake
You could move the magnet out of the coil.

Shanika
Just rotate the magnet through 180° then move it out of the coil.

(a) Which student gave the correct way to reverse the current? Put a tick (✓) in the box next to the correct name. **[1]**

Jessie ◯   Sonny ◯   Jake ◯   Shanika ◯

(b) Which **two** students gave a way to increase the current? Put ticks (✓) in the boxes next to the two correct names. **[1]**

Jessie ◯   Sonny ◯   Jake ◯   Shanika ◯

6 Imran used the following circuit to carry out an experiment to find out what was in the mystery box. He measured the current and calculated the resistance for a range of temperatures. His results are shown in the table.

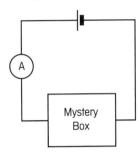

Temperature (°C)	100	80	60	40	20	0
Resistance (Ω)	50	62.5	83.3	125	250	260

(a) (i) What component might have been in the box? .... **[1]**

(ii) What conclusion can be drawn from the table about the relationship between resistance and temperature? **[1]**

....

(b) The reading at 0°C doesn't fit the pattern. What mistake might Imran have made? **[1]**

....

(c) How could the circuit be changed to act as a simple fire alarm? **[1]**

....

HT 7 Explain how, when an alternating potential difference is applied across a primary coil of a transformer, it's possible to obtain an alternating potential difference of a higher value across the secondary coil. **[6]**

✐ *The quality of written communication will be assessed in your answer to this question.*

....
....
....
....
....
....
....
....

8 A transformer has a primary coil of 3000 turns and is connected to a 150V alternating supply. If the output voltage is 900V, how many turns are there on the secondary coil? **[1]**

....
....

P6 Radioactive Materials

Atoms and Elements

All **elements** are made of **atoms**; each element contains only one type of atom. All atoms contain a **nucleus** and **electrons**.

The nucleus is made from **protons** and **neutrons**. Hydrogen (the lightest element) is the one exception; it has no neutrons, just one proton and one electron.

Helium Atom

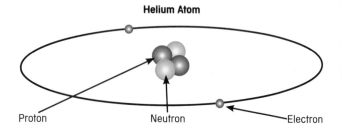

Proton   Neutron   Electron

Radioactive elements emit ionising radiation all the time. Neither chemical reactions nor physical processes (e.g. smelting) can change the radioactive behaviour of a substance.

(HT) Every atom of a **particular element** always has the same number of protons. (If it contained a different number of protons, it would be a different element.) For example…
- hydrogen atoms have one proton
- helium atoms have two protons
- oxygen atoms have eight protons.

But some atoms of the same element can have **different numbers of neutrons** – these are isotopes. For example, there are three isotopes of oxygen:

| Oxygen-16 | Oxygen-17 | Oxygen-18 |
| has eight neutrons | has nine neutrons | has 10 neutrons. |

N.B. All three of these isotopes have eight protons.

Ionising Radiation

Radioactive materials can give out three types of ionising radiation:
- **Alpha**
- **Beta**
- **Gamma**.

Different radioactive materials will give out any one, or a combination, of these radiations.

The different types of radiation have different penetrating powers.

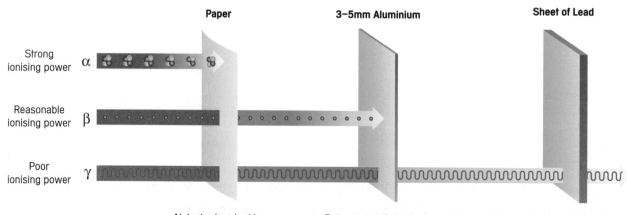

Alpha is absorbed by a few centimetres of air or a thin sheet of paper.

Beta passes through air and paper but is absorbed by a few millimetres of aluminium.

Gamma is very penetrating and needs many centimetres of lead or many metres of concrete to absorb most of it.

Key Words Element • Atom • Nucleus • Electron • Proton • Neutron • Isotope • Alpha • Beta • Gamma

HT Radioactive Decay

Ionising radiation is emitted when the nucleus of an unstable atom decays. The type of **radioactive decay** depends on why the nucleus is unstable; the process of decay helps the atom become more **stable**. During decay the number of protons may change. If this happens the element **changes** to another type.

α decay 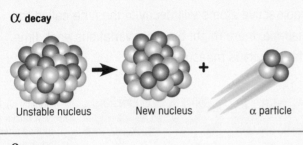 Unstable nucleus — New nucleus + α particle	The original atom decays by ejecting an **alpha (α) particle** from the nucleus. This particle is a **helium nucleus**: a particle made of two protons and two neutrons. With **alpha decay** a new atom is formed. This new atom has two protons and two neutrons fewer than the original.
β decay 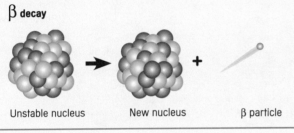 Unstable nucleus — New nucleus + β particle	The original atom decays by changing a neutron into a proton and an electron. This high energy electron, which is now ejected from the nucleus, is a **beta (β) particle**. With **beta decay** a new atom is formed. This new atom has one more proton and one less neutron than the original.
γ decay 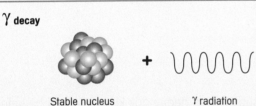 Stable nucleus + γ radiation	After α or β decay, a nucleus sometimes contains surplus energy. It emits this as **gamma (γ) radiation** (very high frequency electromagnetic radiation). During gamma decay, only energy is emitted. This decay doesn't change the type of atom.

Background Radiation

Radioactive elements are found naturally in the environment and contribute to **background radiation**. If a person is *irradiated*, they're exposed to radiation. If they're **contaminated**, then radioactive material is on their skin, clothes or has entered their body.

Nothing can stop us being irradiated and contaminated by background radiation, but generally the levels are so low it's nothing to worry about. However, there appears to be a **correlation** between certain cancers and living in particular areas, especially among people who have lived in granite buildings for many years.

Sources of Background Radiation

Radon gas
Released at surface of ground from uranium in rocks and soil.

From food

Medical
Mainly X-rays.

γ rays
From rocks, soil and building materials.

Cosmic rays
From outer space and the Sun.

Nuclear industry

P6 Radioactive Materials

Measuring the Half-life

As a radioactive atom decays, its activity drops. This means that its radioactivity decreases over time.

The **half-life** of a substance is the time it takes for its radioactivity to halve.

Different substances have different half-lives, ranging from a few seconds to thousands of years.

Experiments to measure the half-life of radioactive elements need to be **repeated** several times and the activity levels for each experiment averaged to give more **reliable** data. Whilst half the number of radioactive atoms will decay in the time called the half-life, there might be slight variations each time the activity is measured.

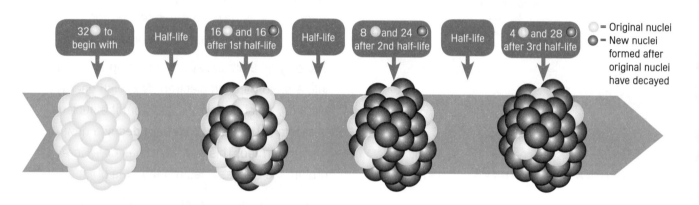

| 32 to begin with | Half-life | 16 and 16 after 1st half-life | Half-life | 8 and 24 after 2nd half-life | Half-life | 4 and 28 after 3rd half-life |

○ = Original nuclei
● = New nuclei formed after original nuclei have decayed

Half-life and Safety

A substance is considered safe once its activity drops to the same level as background radiation. This is a dose of around 3 **millisieverts** per year or 25 counts per minute with a standard detector.

Some substances decay quickly and could be safe in a very short time. Those with a long half-life remain harmful for thousands of years.

HT Half-life Calculations

The half-life can be used to calculate how old a radioactive substance is, or how long it will take to become safe.

Example

If a sample has an activity of 800 counts per minute and a half-life of 2 hours, how many hours will it take for the activity to reach the background rate of 25 counts per minute?

We need to work out how many half-lives it takes for the sample of 800 counts to reach 25 counts.

1. $\dfrac{800}{2} = 400$ 2. $\dfrac{400}{2} = 200$ 3. $\dfrac{200}{2} = 100$ 4. $\dfrac{100}{2} = 50$ 5. $\dfrac{50}{2} = 25$

It takes 5 half-lives to reach a count of 25, and each half-life takes 2 hours.

So, it takes 5 × 2 hours = **10 hours**

Half-life

Dangers of Radiation

Ionising radiation can break molecules into ions. These ions can damage living cells and the cells may be killed or become cancerous.

(HT) Ions are **very reactive** and can take part in other chemical reactions.

Many jobs involve using radioactive materials (e.g. workers in nuclear power stations, radiographers, etc.). People can become **irradiated** or **contaminated**, so their exposure needs to be carefully monitored.

Different types of radiation carry different risks:
- **Alpha** is the most dangerous if the source is **inside the body**; all the radiation will be absorbed by cells in the body.
- **Beta** is the most dangerous if the source is **outside the body**. Unlike alpha, it can penetrate the outer layer of skin and damage internal organs.
- **Gamma** can cause harm if it's absorbed by the cells, but it is weakly ionising and can pass straight through the body causing no damage at all.

The **sievert** is a measure of a radiation dose's potential to harm a person. It's based on both the type and the amount of radiation absorbed.

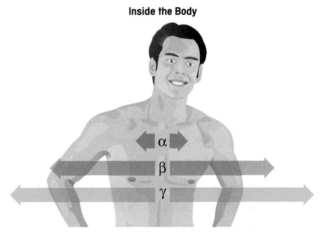

Inside the Body

Outside the Body

Uses of Radiation

Although using ionising radiation can be dangerous, there are many beneficial uses.

High-energy gamma rays in **cancer treatment** can destroy cancer cells but can damage healthy cells too. The radiation has to be carefully targeted from different angles to minimise the damage. Doctors need to carefully weigh the **risks** against the benefits before going ahead.

Radiation is also used in the following ways:
- To **sterilise surgical instruments** and to **sterilise food**. This kills bacteria.
- As a tracer in the body, for example in **PET** (**Positron Emission Tomography**) scans.

(HT) In PET scans, radio-labelled glucose is injected into the patient's bloodstream, from which it is absorbed into the tissues, as glucose is needed for respiration. A pair of gamma ray photons is emitted from the radio-labelled glucose in active cells. These are detected by gamma ray cameras and used to produce an image, for instance of the brain, showing any abnormal regions. Cancerous cells often absorb more glucose, so they will emit more gamma rays than surrounding tissues and will be detected.

In radiotherapy, a beam of gamma rays is focused from different angles onto cancer cells to destroy them. This gives a concentrated dose to the cancer cells but a smaller dose to the surrounding tissue.

P6 Radioactive Materials

Nuclear Waste

Nuclear power stations release energy due to changes in the **nucleus** of radioactive substances. They don't produce carbon dioxide but they do produce radioactive waste.

Nuclear waste is categorised into three types:

- **High-level waste** (HLW) – very radioactive waste that has to be stored carefully. Fortunately, only small amounts are produced and it doesn't remain radioactive for long, so it's put into short-term storage.
- **Intermediate-level waste** (ILW) – not as radioactive as HLW but it remains radioactive for thousands of years. Increasing amounts are produced; deciding how to store it is a problem. At the moment most ILW is mixed with concrete and stored in big containers, but this isn't a permanent solution.
- **Low-level waste** (LLW) – only slightly radioactive waste that is sealed and placed in landfills.

Nuclear power stations...

- don't emit smoke from chimneys as happens in fossil-fuel power stations
- don't release greenhouse gases into the atmosphere.

Spent fuel rods from the reactors in nuclear power stations...

- still contain 90% uranium
- are sent away to be reprocessed and used to make new fuel rods
- are examples of high-level waste.

If you were standing within a few metres of unprotected spent fuel rods, you would receive a lethal dose of radiation in a few seconds.

This table shows risks related to radiation dose:

Situation	Dose (millisieverts)	Risk to Health
Dental X-ray	0.1	Very low
Background radiation per year	3	Safe
Computerised Tomography (CT) scan	15	Considered an acceptable risk
Exposure to medium radioactive waste	100	Lowest level that causes a measured increased risk of cancer
Inside the tsunami and earthquake-damaged nuclear plant in Fukushima, Japan, in 2011	400	Serious risk of developing cancer

Quick Test

1. What particles are found in the nucleus?
2. Name the three types of ionising radiation.
3. What is the type of radiation that passes through paper but is stopped by 3mm of aluminium?
4. Give two sources of background radiation.
5. What is meant by the term 'half-life'?
6. **HT** Describe an alpha particle.
7. **HT** A radioactive source has an activity of 288 counts per minute and a half-life of 6 hours. What will the activity be after 24 hours?
8. **HT** If a radioactive nucleus emits a beta particle, how does the nucleus change?

HT Nuclear Fission

In a **chemical reaction** it's the electrons that cause the change. The elements involved stay the same but join up in different ways.

Nuclear fission takes place in the nucleus of the atom and different elements are formed:

- A **neutron** is absorbed by a large and unstable uranium nucleus. This splits the nucleus into two roughly equal-sized, smaller nuclei. This releases energy and more neutrons.
- A fission reaction releases far more energy than even the most **exothermic** chemical reactions. Once fission has taken place, the neutrons can be absorbed by other nuclei and further fission reactions can take place. This is a chain reaction.
- A chain reaction occurs when there's enough **fissile material** to prevent too many neutrons escaping without being absorbed. This is called **critical mass** and ensures every reaction triggers at least one further reaction.

Only uranium and plutonium can undergo nuclear fission in this way.

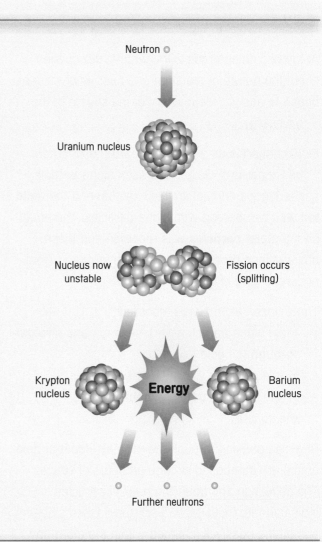

Neutron

Uranium nucleus

Nucleus now unstable | Fission occurs (splitting)

Krypton nucleus | **Energy** | Barium nucleus

Further neutrons

The Nuclear Reactor

Nuclear power stations use fission reactions to generate the heat needed to produce **steam**. The nuclear reactor controls the chain reaction so that the energy is steadily released.

Fission occurs in the **fuel rods** and causes them to become very hot.

The **coolant** is a fluid pumped through the reactor. The coolant heats up and is then used in the **heat exchanger** to turn water into steam.

Control rods, made of **boron**, absorb neutrons, preventing the chain reaction getting out of control. Moving the control rods in and out of the **reactor core** changes the amount of fission that takes place.

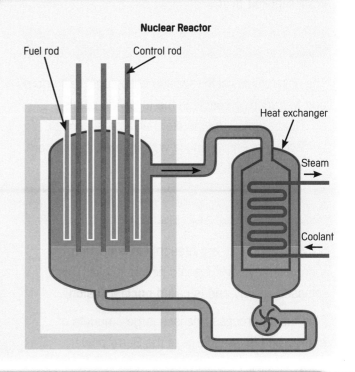

Nuclear Reactor

Fuel rod | Control rod

Heat exchanger

Steam

Coolant

P6 Radioactive Materials

Alpha Particle Scattering Experiment

At the beginning of the 20th century, discoveries about the nature of the atom and nuclear processes began to answer the mystery of the source of the Sun's energy.

In 1911, there was a ground-breaking experiment – the Rutherford–Geiger–Marsden alpha particle scattering experiment. In this experiment a thin **gold foil** was bombarded with alpha particles. The effect on the **alpha particles** was recorded and these observations provided the evidence for our current understanding of atoms.

Three observations were recorded:
- Most alpha particles were seen to **pass straight through** the gold foil.
- Some particles were **deflected** slightly.
- A few particles **bounced back** towards the source.

Particles passing through the foil indicated that gold atoms are composed of large amounts of space. The deflection and bouncing back of particles indicated that these alpha particles passed close to something positively charged within the atom and were repelled by it.

The Gold Foil Scattering Experiment

Alpha particle

Most particles passed straight through

Some particles were deflected back

Gold atom

Some particles were deflected slightly

Conclusions of the Experiment

The observations of this experiment brought Rutherford and Marsden to conclude the following points:
- Gold atoms, and therefore all atoms, consist largely of empty space with a small, dense core. They called this core the nucleus.
- The nucleus is positively charged.
- The **electrons** are arranged around the nucleus with a great deal of space between them.

The Nucleus of an Atom

If hydrogen nuclei are brought close enough together, they can fuse into helium nuclei. This releases energy and is called **nuclear fusion**.

This fusion process releases large amounts of energy and is the source of the Sun's power.

> (HT) We now know that the nucleus contains **positive protons** and **neutral neutrons** held together by the short-ranged **strong nuclear force**. This force balances the repulsive electrostatic force between the protons.

Nucleus • Electron

Nuclear Energy

The amount of energy released during nuclear fission is much greater than that released in a chemical reaction involving a similar mass of material.

(HT) Einstein's equation states that for a mass of matter, **m**, the amount of energy, **E**, produced during nuclear fusion or fission is given by:

$$E = mc^2 \quad \text{where } c \text{ is the speed of light in a vacuum}$$

Example 1

How much energy was generated from a uranium fuel rod if 2kg of the fuel was 'used up' during the fission process?

Using $E = mc^2$

$$E = 2 \times (3 \times 10^8)^2$$
$$= 2 \times 9 \times 10^{16}$$
$$= \textbf{18} \times \textbf{10}^{\textbf{16}} \textbf{ joules}$$

Example 2

How much energy is released in the Sun, from the fusion of hydrogen atoms to form one helium atom, if the loss of mass is 4.75×10^{-29}kg?

Using $E = mc^2$

$$E = 4.75 \times 10^{-29} \times (3 \times 10^8)^2$$
$$= 4.75 \times 10^{-29} \times 9 \times 10^{16}$$
$$= \textbf{4.28} \times \textbf{10}^{\textbf{-12}} \textbf{ joules}$$

(HT) Nuclear Equations

A radium nucleus decays by emitting an alpha particle. A new element is formed, which is called radon:

$$^{226}_{88}\text{Ra} \longrightarrow ^{222}_{86}\text{Rn} + ^{4}_{2}\text{He}$$

A **radioactive** carbon nucleus decays by emitting a beta particle:

$$^{14}_{6}\text{C} \longrightarrow ^{14}_{7}\text{N} + ^{0}_{-1}\text{e}$$

Note that gamma rays are just a form of energy. They don't change either the **atomic number**, or the mass number, when released from a radioactive nucleus.

Quick Test

1. How is intermediate-level waste stored?
2. What particles were used to bombard the gold foil in the Rutherford–Geiger–Marsden experiment?
3. What conclusion was made about the nucleus from the Rutherford–Geiger–Marsden experiment?
4. (HT) What element is used in control rods in a nuclear reactor?
5. (HT) What elements can be used in a nuclear power station fuel rod?

P6 Exam Practice Questions

1. Four students are talking about ionising radiation.

Melanie
I live in an area with high radon gas, which is a concern.

Dol
Ionising radiation comes from the nucleus of unstable atoms.

Nathan
Gamma can be used to treat cancer.

Liam
Alpha is easily absorbed by cells.

(a) Which **two** students are considering the risks of ionising radiation? Put ticks (✓) in the boxes next to the two correct answers. [1]

Melanie ◯ Dol ◯ Nathan ◯ Liam ◯

(b) Which **two** students are talking about sources of background radiation? Put ticks (✓) in the boxes next to the two correct answers. [1]

Melanie ◯ Dol ◯ Nathan ◯ Liam ◯

2. Draw a straight line from each term to the statement that best explains the term. [2]

Term	Statement
Half-life	Measurement of a radiation dose's potential to harm a patient
Sievert	Rate of emission of radiation from the nucleus
Activity	Measurement of the time it takes for activity to drop by a half

3. Rutherford, Geiger and Marsden carried out an alpha particle scattering experiment with gold. Explain what conclusions they came to about atoms as a result of the experiment. [6]

🖉 *The quality of written communication will be assessed in your answer to this question.*

4 Nuclear power stations are still seen as a main source of energy in the UK but a nuclear reactor will need fuel rods to be replaced when they still contain 90% uranium.

(a) Give one advantage and one disadvantage of nuclear power stations. **[2]**

(b) Why are spent fuel rods sent away to be reprocessed rather than treated as nuclear waste? **[1]**

HT 5 **(a)** What is a chain reaction? **[6]**

✏ *The quality of written communication will be assessed in your answer to this question.*

(b) There are several isotopes of uranium. What is an isotope? **[1]**

(c) An isotope of uranium has an atomic number of 92 and a mass number 238. It decays by emitting an alpha particle. What will be the atomic number and mass number of the element formed as a result of the decay? **[1]**

(d) During the nuclear decay of uranium, the mass decreases by 0.05g. How much energy was released? **[2]**

(e) In an atomic nucleus, there is a strong repulsive force between the protons and the neutrons. Why doesn't the nucleus disintegrate? **[1]**

Answers

Module B4: The Processes of Life

Quick Test Answers

Page 7

1. (They contain the enzymes for) aerobic respiration.
2. Cell wall, chloroplasts and permanent vacuole
3. Protein molecules that speed up reactions in cells / act as catalysts in living things.
4. The release of energy (from food chemicals) in all living cells.
5. Anaerobic respiration doesn't use oxygen, whereas aerobic does use oxygen.
6. Denatured

Page 11

1. Chlorophyll
2. Oxygen
3. Nitrates
4. **Any one from:** A random section across an area; A representative area to sample.
5. The movement of substances from a region of high concentration to an area of low concentration.
6. Water

Exam Practice Answers

1. **(a) (i)** C **(ii)** D
   (b) They contain the enzymes for (aerobic) respiration.
2. **(a)** The greater the light intensity, the faster the rate of photosynthesis.
   (b) Oxygen
   (c) Any one from: Carbon dioxide; Temperature
3. Ethanol is produced as a waste product **should be ticked**.
4. **(a) Any one from:** To ensure that they weren't different; To ensure they were the same type/consistency; To ensure they didn't 'react' differently.
   (b) Water had entered the potato (cells).
   (c) Water had moved out of the potato (cells).
5. **(a)** Oxygen; Carbon dioxide; Dissolved food
   (b) partially; dilute; concentrated; osmosis **[2 marks if four correct; 1 mark if two correct]**
6. **(a)** Sebastian; Nicholas
   (b) It's where an enzyme is permanently destroyed and stops working.

Module B5: Growth and Development

Quick Test Answers

Page 17

1. A group of similar cells (to perform a function).
2. Mitosis
3. Testes and ovaries
4. Zygote
5. bases
6. Messenger RNA / mRNA

Page 21

1. Meristems
2. Xylem (vessels)
3. Phloem
4. Hormone / Auxin
5. Phototropism

Exam Practice Answers

1. **(a)** [B | D | C | A]
   [1 mark for D before C; 1 mark for C before A]
   (b) Testes; Ovaries
   (c) Zygote

2. **This is a model answer which would score full marks:** The Sun shining on the plant from only one side would mean that it would grow towards the light. This is because the growth rate on the dark side is much faster than on the light side. This pattern of growth is called phototropism and is caused by hormones. It helps the plant to obtain more sunlight energy for photosynthesis. This allows the plant to produce more glucose, giving it more energy for growth and reproduction, and helping it to survive.
   A good answer could also include the following point: Auxin being destroyed by light, promoting growth on the dark side.
3. **(a)** They're unspecialised and can turn into any kind of cell.
   (b) The cells will have become specialised.
   (c) Embryonic stem cells can develop into any specialised cell, whereas adult stem cells can only develop into some specialised cells.
4. **(a) Any two from:** B quadruples every 30 minutes, whereas D does not; The growth of B is constant, whereas D changes; The growth of B is faster than D; B has 12 division cycles, whereas D has 10 cycles.
   (b) (In all four cases the number quadrupled in this time). **Any one from:** B / D also quadrupled between 0 and 30 minutes; D also quadrupled between 90 and 120 minutes and/or between 150 and 180 minutes; B quadrupled every time.
5. **(a)** Chloe; Emily
   (b) mRNA is a smaller copy that is small enough to leave.

Module B6: Brain and Mind

Quick Test Answers
Page 27
1. A change in an organism's environment.
2. Motor neuron
3. Synapse
4. Axon
5. A fast, automatic, involuntary response to a stimulus.
6. Conditioned reflex action

Page 31
1. Neuron pathways
2. Cerebral cortex
3. MRI (Magnetic Resonance Imaging)
4. The ability to store and retrieve information.
5. Short-term memory
6. They affect the passage of an impulse across a synapse.

Exam Practice Answers
1. (a) (i) central nervous system **should be ringed**.
   (ii) peripheral nervous system **should be ringed**.
   (b) (i) Sensory neuron
   (ii) Motor neuron
   (c) It causes the gland to release a hormone into the blood.
   (d) It insulates the neuron; It increases the speed at which the impulse travels.

(e) Synapses are the gaps between adjacent neurons.
(f) They change the speed at which nerve impulses travel to the brain.

2. **This is a model answer which would score full marks:** When Raul picks up the plate, receptors in his skin will be stimulated to set up an impulse in a sensory neuron. This impulse will move across a synapse to a relay neuron in his spinal cord and then across a second synapse to set up an impulse in a motor neuron. This impulse will pass to muscles in his arm, causing contraction, resulting in him moving his fingers to release the hot plate.
   A good answer could also include the following point: Neurotransmitters also diffuse across the synapse.
3. (a) 1.32 in small dose
   (b) The drug slows down the reaction time.
   (c) **Any one from:** So that it's a good estimate of the true reaction time; Repeatability reduces the chances of a false result. [**Do not accept 'to make it a fair test'.**]
4. have a scientific mechanism; be published; **and** be repeatable **should be ticked. [2 marks for all three; 1 mark for two]**
5. (a) [D | B | E | C | A] **[1 mark for B before E; 1 mark for E before C; 1 mark for C before A]**
   (b) Ecstasy (MDMA)

Module C4: Chemical Patterns

Quick Test Answers
Page 36
1. They all have similar physical and chemical properties, and they all have one electron in their outer shell.
2. (a) A mass of 1 and a charge of +1.
   (b) Almost zero mass and a charge of -1.
   (c) A mass of 1 and no charge (it's neutral).

Page 39
1. Melting point decreases and reactivity increases going down the group.
2. They react with water to produce alkaline hydroxide solutions.
3. It floats, fizzes and moves around the surface of the water. Hydrogen and potassium hydroxide are produced. The gas ignites to give a purple flame.
4. Its outer electron is further from the nucleus, so it's held less strongly and lost more easily.

Page 43
1. Lithium is the odd one out because the other elements are halogens.
2. The melting point increases and the reactivity decreases.
3. Potassium bromide and iodine
4. Lithium fluoride

Exam Practice Answers
1. (a)

Particle	Relative Mass	Relative Charge
Proton	1	+
Neutron	1	0 / No charge / Neutral
Electron	Negligible	−

[1 mark for each correct row]
   (b) (i) Nucleus
   (ii) Electron / Electron shell
   (c) The number of protons in an atom.

(d) (i) Sophie **should be ringed**.
   (ii) Chlorine + Sodium $\longrightarrow$ Sodium chloride **[1 mark for correct reactants (in either order); 1 mark for correctly named product (not 'NaCl').]**
2. (a) The alkali metals
   (b)

Element	Melting Point (K)	Boiling Point (K)	Formula of Chloride
Lithium	453	Accept any answer from 1250–1350	LiCl
Sodium	370	1156	**NaCl**
Potassium	Accept any answer from 280–350	1032	KCl

(c) **Any two from:** It floats; Gas is produced; It moves around on the surface; There is a vigorous reaction.
   Sodium + Water $\longrightarrow$ Sodium hydroxide + Hydrogen **[1]**
   pH 11/12/13/14 **[1]**
(d) Flammable **[1]**. Keep away from sources of ignition / heat / fire / Bunsen burner **[1]**.
3. (a) Protons: 9; Electrons: 9; Neutrons: 10
   (b) $F_2(g) + 2Na(s) \longrightarrow 2NaF(s)$
   [1 mark for correct formulae of products and reactants; 1 mark for correct state symbols; 1 mark for a balanced equation.]
   (c) **This is a model answer which would score full marks:** At the start of the experiment, the lamp wouldn't light up because ionic substances don't conduct electricity when solid. This is because the ions are fixed in place. As the solid lead fluoride melts, the ions would become free to move and so the molten lead fluoride would conduct electricity. Therefore the lamp would light up.

Answers

Module C5: Chemicals of the Natural Environment

Quick Test Answers
Page 48
1. The hydrosphere is the term used for the water and dissolved salts on Earth.
2. 21%
3. **Any two from:** It has a high melting point; It's hard; It's insoluble in water.
4. **Any two from:** They have a high melting point; They have a high boiling point; They don't conduct when solid; They conduct when molten or if dissolved.

Page 53
1. Add sodium hydroxide solution and see what colour the precipitate is.
2. Add barium nitrate solution. A white precipitate identifies sulfate ions.
3. The positive ions move towards the negative electrode where they gain electrons. The negative ions move towards the positive electrode where they lose electrons.
4. Positive electrode: oxygen
   Negative electrode: aluminium
5. $Fe^{3+}(aq) + 3OH^-(aq) \longrightarrow Fe(OH)_3(s)$

Exam Practice Answers
1. **(a)** Add sodium hydroxide solution to test for copper ions **[1]** and expect to see a blue precipitate **[1]**. Add silver nitrate solution to test for chloride ions **[1]** and expect to see a white precipitate **[1]**.

(b) Carbonate ion **[1]**. Carbon dioxide **[1]**.
2. **(a)** The ions are able to move apart **[1]** and change to a random arrangement / gain energy / move faster **[1]**.
   (b) oxygen; bottom / cathode; oxygen; top **[2 marks for all four correct; 1 mark for two correct.]**
   (c) This is a model answer which would score full marks:
   Aluminium is used for saucepans because it's a good conductor of heat and has a high melting point. Metals have high melting points because of the strong forces of attraction in the lattice structure. Aluminium is used for power lines because it's strong and conducts electricity well. Aluminium is used in aeroplanes because it's strong and lightweight and doesn't corrode. Aluminium is strong because of the tightly packed crystal lattice structure.
   A good answer using higher tier understanding could include the following points: Aluminium is malleable because the rows of ions can slide over each other; Aluminium conducts electricity because the delocalised electrons are free to move in one direction when a voltage is applied.
3. **(a)** $Zn^{2+}(aq) + CO_3^{2-}(aq) \longrightarrow ZnCO_3(s)$
   [1 mark for correct charge on zinc ion; 1 mark for correct formulae and balancing; 1 mark for correct state symbols.]
   (b) $Cu^{2+}(aq) + 2OH^-(aq) \longrightarrow Cu(OH)_2(s)$
   [1 mark for correct formula of $Cu(OH)_2$; 1 mark for correct balancing; 1 mark for correct state symbols.]

Module C6: Chemical Synthesis

Quick Test Answers
Page 59
1. Toxic: skull and crossbones
   Flammable: a flame
2. HCl is hydrochloric acid and H_2SO_4 is sulfuric acid.
3. NaOH
4. $MgO + 2HNO_3 \longrightarrow Mg(NO_3)_2 + H_2O$

Page 63
1. 84
2. 75%
3. **Any three from:** Crystallisation; Filtration; Evaporation; Drying in an oven or desiccator
4. Using a titration
5. 88kg

Page 67
1. The amount of product made per unit time.
2. By weighing the reaction mixture; Measuring the volume of gas produced; Observing the formation of a precipitate.
3. To make the chemical more quickly, so that more profit could be made.
4. The reactant particles are closer together, so the collisions are more frequent.
5. Powders have a larger surface area, so collisions are more frequent.
6. **Any three from:** Catalysts speed up reactions; Catalysts aren't used up or chemically changed; Different reactions need different catalysts; Catalysts lower the activation energy.

Exam Practice Answers
1. **(a) Accept any answer between 1 and 6.**
   (b) Citric acid + Sodium hydrogencarbonate $\longrightarrow$ Sodium citrate **+ Water + Carbon dioxide**

(c) (i) Magnesium + Hydrochloric acid $\longrightarrow$ Magnesium chloride **[1]** + Hydrogen **[1]**
   (ii) Hydrogen is flammable **[accept 'magnesium chloride may be harmful'.]**
   (iii) Calcium carbonate + Hydrochloric acid $\longrightarrow$ Calcium chloride + Water + Carbon dioxide **[1]**
   Magnesium carbonate + Hydrochloric acid $\longrightarrow$ Magnesium chloride + Water + Carbon dioxide **[1]**
   The products of these reactions aren't toxic or flammable **[1]**.
   A good answer could also include the following point: Both calcium carbonate and magnesium carbonate are insoluble, so if you take too much antacid it will not make your stomach alkaline.
2. **(a) (i)** Hydrogen / H^+
   (ii) Hydroxide / OH^-
   (iii) $H^+(aq) + OH^-(aq) \longrightarrow H_2O(l)$
   [1 mark for correct reactants and product; 1 mark for correct state symbols.]

(b)

A	C	E	B	D	F	G

[3 marks for all four correct; if incorrect, C before E scores 1 mark, and B before D scores 1 mark.]
3. **(a)** 21–22cm³
   (b) Any two from: Increase the concentration of the acid; Increase the surface area of the magnesium carbonate / grind up the magnesium carbonate; Increase the temperature **[accept 'add a catalyst'.]**
   (c) RFM of $MgCO_3$ is 84 **[1]** and RFM of $Mg(NO_3)_2$ is 148 **[1]**. So 8.4g of $MgCO_3$ will make 14.8g of $Mg(NO_3)_2$ **[1]**.

Module P4: Explaining Motion

Quick Test Answers
Page 72
1. It was zero – the speed was constant.
2. 20m North

Page 79
1. Action
2. 24kg m/s
3. Crumple zone; Seat belt; Air bag
4. $\frac{1}{2} \times 60 \times 4^2 = 480$J
5. 20m
6. 4m/s

Exam Practice Answers
1. **(a)** A3; B2; C1 **[2 marks for all three correct, 1 mark for one correct]**
   (b) The speed
2. **(a)** 8m/s **should be ringed**.
   (b) 7.5m/s^2 **should be ringed**.
3. Speed–time graphs are used in lorry tachographs to make sure drivers rest for the appropriate time **and** Friction is a force that always opposes motion **should be ticked**.
4. **This is a model answer which would score full marks:** Without friction it would be impossible to walk. There is a frictional force that is experienced by the shoe and acts in the direction the person is walking in. The force experienced by the pavement is in the opposite direction and has the same magnitude. As the person wearing the shoe has a much smaller mass than the ground, the person moves forward relative to the ground.

5. **(a)** Momentum = 1500 × 45 = 67 500kg m/s
   [1 mark for correct working but wrong answer]
   (b) Acceleration = $\frac{55 - 45}{4}$ = 2.5m/s^2
   [1 mark for correct working but wrong answer]
6. The change in momentum depends on the size of the force acting and the time it acts for **and** If the resultant force on a car is zero, its momentum is constant **should be ticked**.
7. PE lost = Weight × Height
   $\quad\quad\quad$ = 40 × 20 = 800J
   PE lost = KE gained
   $\quad$ 800 = $\frac{1}{2}mv^2$
   $\quad$ 800 = $\frac{1}{2} \times 4 \times v^2$
   $\quad\quad$ v = 20m/s
   [1 mark for correct working but wrong answer]
8. **(a)** Change in momentum = 150 × 3 – (150 × -2) (Remember the velocity of rebound will be negative.)
   Change in momentum = 450 + 300 = 750kg m/s
   [1 mark for correct working but wrong answer]
   (b) Force × 0.5 = 750, so force = 1500N
   [1 mark for correct working but wrong answer]
   (c) To increase the impact time, which reduces the force on his body.

Module P5: Electric Circuits

Quick Test Answers
Page 85
1. Positive
2.
3. 4Ω
4. They're proportional.
5. 0.5A
6. There are more collisions between the flowing electrons and the vibrating ions, giving a higher resistance. This leads to more heat being produced by the resistor.

Page 89
1. The principle of electromagnetic induction.
2. 6W
3. A changing magnetic field.
4. 4000 turns
5. 0.25A

Exam Practice Answers
1. The two rods will attract each other.
2. ⊣⊢ **should be ringed**.
3. Lamp – 2A; Reslstor – 30V; Coil – 6Ω

4. **Any two from:** Spin the magnet faster; Increase the number of turns on the coil; Use a stronger magnet.
5. **(a)** Jake **should be ticked**.
   (b) Jessie **and** Sonny **should be ticked**. **[Both needed for 1 mark.]**
6. **(a) (i)** Thermistor
   (ii) They're inversely proportional. **[Accept 'there is a negative correlation'.]**
   (b) Any one from: Read the ammeter incorrectly; Not put the thermistor in the ice; Not measured the temperature correctly.
   (c) Add a buzzer or bell in series with the battery and thermistor (and ammeter).
7. **This is a model answer which would score full marks:** An alternating potential difference across the primary coil produces an alternating magnetic field in the iron core. This alternating field passes backwards and forwards around the iron core and through the secondary coil, which has more turns than the primary coil. This induces an alternating potential difference across the secondary coil which will be higher than the input alternating voltage.
8. $\frac{3000}{\text{Secondary turns}} = \frac{150}{900}$

   So secondary turns = 18 000

Answers

Quick Test Answers
Page 96
1. Protons and neutrons
2. Alpha; Beta; Gamma
3. Beta
4. **Any two from:** Radon gas; Medical; Food; Cosmic rays; Gamma rays; Nuclear industry
5. The time it takes for the radioactivity to halve.
6. An alpha particle is a helium nucleus and consists of two protons and two neutrons.
7. 18 counts per minute.
8. It has one more proton and one less neutron than the original nucleus.

Page 99
1. It is mixed with concrete and stored in big containers.
2. Alpha particles
3. Gold atoms (and therefore all atoms) consisted of mainly empty space with a small, dense core called the nucleus. The charge on the nucleus was positive.
4. Boron
5. Uranium or plutonium

Exam Practice Answers
1. (a) Melanie **and** Liam **should be ticked. [Both needed for 1 mark.]**
   (b) Melanie **and** Dol **should be ticked. [Both needed for 1 mark.]**
2. Half-life – Measurement of the time it takes for activity to drop by a half
   Sievert – Measurement of a radiation dose's potential to harm a person
   Activity – Rate of emission of radiation from the nucleus
   [2 marks for all three correct; 1 mark for one correct.]
3. **This is a model answer which would score full marks:**
   They concluded that an atom mostly consisted of empty space (a vacuum) because most alpha particles passed straight through the gold foil. The electrons were arranged around the nucleus of the atom with a great deal of space between them. Only some of the alpha particles were deflected or bounced back, suggesting that the nucleus was small, dense and positively charged. This made it difficult for alpha particles to knock out or interact with the nucleus.

4. (a) Advantage: **Any one from:** They don't produce carbon dioxide; They don't produce sulfur dioxide; They don't produce particulates.
   Disadvantage: **Any one from:** They produce radioactive waste; Risk of serious accident.
   (b) It makes sense to recycle the uranium and cut down on the radioactive waste that needs to be disposed of. **[Accept that it reduces the need to remove extra uranium from the ground.]**
5. (a) **This is a model answer which would score full marks:** A chain reaction is when a uranium (or plutonium) nucleus absorbs a neutron, becoming unstable. It then splits into two smaller nuclei, releasing energy and producing three more neutrons. There is enough fissile material to prevent too many neutrons escaping without being absorbed. This is the critical mass and ensures every reaction triggers at least one further reaction.
   (b) An isotope of an element has the same number of protons (atomic number) as that element but a different number of neutrons.
   (c) The atomic number will be 90 and the mass number will be 234. **[Both must be correct for 1 mark.]**
   (d) $E = mc^2 = \dfrac{0.05}{1000} \times (3 \times 10^8)^2 = 4.5 \times 10^{12}\text{J}$
   [1 mark for correct working but wrong answer].
   (e) The strong nuclear force opposes and balances the force of repulsion.

Acceleration – the rate at which an object increases in speed.

Acid – a compound that has a pH value lower than 7.

Activation energy – the minimum amount of energy required to cause a reaction.

Aerobic respiration – respiration using oxygen; releases energy and produces carbon dioxide and water.

Air resistance – the opposition to motion due to air friction.

Alkali – a compound that has a pH value higher than 7 and is soluble in water.

Alkali metals – the six metals in Group 1 of the periodic table.

Alpha – a radioactive particle made of two protons and two neutrons.

Alternating current – an electric current that changes direction of flow continuously.

Anaerobic respiration – the process of releasing energy from glucose in living cells in the absence of oxygen to produce a small amount of energy very quickly.

Atmosphere – the layer of gas surrounding the Earth.

Atom – the smallest chemical particle of an element.

Axon – the thread-like extension of a nerve cell.

Beta – a type of radioactive particle made of an electron.

Catalyst – a substance that increases the rate of a chemical reaction without being changed itself.

Central nervous system – the brain and spinal cord; allows an organism to react to its surroundings and coordinates its responses.

Cerebral cortex – the part of the human brain most concerned with intelligence, memory, language and consciousness.

Chlorophyll – the green pigment found in most plants; responsible for photosynthesis.

Chromosome – a long molecule found in the nucleus of all cells containing DNA.

Clone – an organism genetically identical to the parent.

Collision theory – a principle that helps to explain rates of reaction. For a reaction to occur, particles must collide with enough energy. Factors that increase the frequency or energy of collisions will speed up a reaction.

Commutator – part of an electric motor which is a segmented disk that rotates with the coil switching over the contacts with the two brushes. This keeps the current flowing in one direction through the magnetic field and ensures rotation of the coil.

Compound – a substance consisting of two or more different elements chemically combined.

Conditioned reflex – a reflex action brought about by a learned stimulus.

Current – the rate of flow of an electrical charge, measured in amperes (A).

Diamond – a form of pure carbon in which each atom is bonded to four other atoms to give a very hard substance.

Diatomic molecule – a molecule that only exists in pairs of atoms.

Diffusion – the net movement of particles from an area of high concentration to an area of low concentration.

Direct current – an electric current that only flows in one direction.

Displacement – the process that occurs during a chemical reaction when a more reactive element will swap places with a less reactive element within a compound.

Distance–time graph – a graph showing distance travelled against time taken; the gradient of the line represents speed.

Glossary of Key Words

DNA (deoxyribonucleic acid) – molecules that code for genetic information and make up chromosomes.

Effector – the part of the body, e.g. a muscle or a gland, which produces a response to a stimulus.

Electrolysis – the process by which an electric current causes a solution to undergo chemical decomposition.

Electrolyte – the molten or aqueous solution of an ionic compound used in electrolysis.

Electron – a negatively charged particle found orbiting the nucleus of an atom.

Electron configuration – the arrangement of electrons in fixed shells / energy levels around the nucleus of an atom of an element.

Element – a substance that consists of one type of atom.

Embryo – a ball of cells that will develop into a human / animal baby.

Endothermic – a chemical reaction that takes in heat from its surroundings so that the products have more energy than the reactants.

Enzyme – a protein that speeds up the rate of reaction in living organisms (a catalyst in living things).

Exothermic – a chemical reaction that gives out energy (heat) to its surroundings so that the products have less energy than the reactants.

Fertilisation – the fusion of the male gamete with the female gamete.

Field lines – lines of force that, by definition, pass from the North pole of a magnet to the South pole.

Force – a push or pull acting upon an object.

Friction – the resistive force between two surfaces as they move over each other.

Gamete – a specialised sex cell formed by meiosis.

Gamma – a radioactive emission that is an electromagnetic wave.

Gene – a small section of DNA of a chromosome that determines a particular characteristic.

Generator – a device in which a magnet spins inside a coil of wire to produce a voltage or an electric current.

Gradient – the steepness of the slope of a graph.

Graphite – a form of pure carbon in which each atom is bonded to three other atoms to create a structure made of sheets that can slide over each other and conduct electricity.

Gravity – a force of attraction between masses; the force that keeps objects orbiting larger objects.

Group – a vertical column of elements in the periodic table.

Half-life – the time taken for half the radioactive atoms in a material to decay.

Halogen – one of the five non-metals in Group 7 of the periodic table.

Hazard – something that can cause harm. In chemistry, hazards are often chemicals and we use symbols to identify different types of hazard, e.g. flammable, corrosive, etc.

Hydrosphere – contains all the water on Earth including rivers, oceans, lakes, etc.

Instantaneous speed – the speed of an object at a particular point.

Ion – a particle that has a positive or negative electrical charge.

Ionic bond – the process by which two or more atoms lose or gain electrons to become charged ions.

Ionic compound – a compound consisting of charged particles called ions. Ionic compounds are (nearly always) made from a metal and a non-metal.

Irradiation – when a person is exposed to radioactive emissions.

Kinetic energy – the energy possessed by an object because of its movement.

Lithosphere – the rigid outer layer of the Earth made up of the crust and the part of the mantle just below it.

Magnetic field – a region where a force acts on a magnetic material placed there.

Meiosis – the cell division that forms daughter cells with half the number of chromosomes as the parent cell.

Memory – the ability to store and retrieve information.

Meristem – an area where unspecialised cells divide, producing plant growth.

Mitosis – the cell division that forms two daughter cells, each with the same number of chromosomes as the parent cell.

Momentum – a measure of state of motion of an object as a product of its mass and velocity.

Neuron – a specialised cell that transmits electrical messages or nerve impulses when stimulated.

Neutralisation – a reaction between an acid and a base that forms a neutral solution.

Neutron – a particle found in the nucleus of atoms that has no electric charge.

Nuclear waste – the radioactive waste left over as a by-product of nuclear power generation.

Nucleus – the small central core of an atom, consisting of protons and neutrons (except hydrogen, which contains a single proton); the control centre of a cell, containing DNA.

Ore – a naturally occurring mineral, from which it's economically viable to extract a metal.

Organ – a collection of tissues to carry out a function.

Organelles – the different parts of a cell's structure.

Osmosis – the movement of water from a dilute to a more concentrated solution across a partially permeable membrane.

Period – a horizontal row of elements in the periodic table.

Photosynthesis – the chemical process that takes place in green plants where water combines with carbon dioxide to produce glucose using light.

Phototropism – a plant's response to light.

Polymer – a large molecule made up from many similar units (monomers).

Potential difference – the work done on or by per unit charge as it passes between two points in a circuit.

Precipitate – the solid formed in a reaction between two liquids.

Precipitation – a type of reaction in which a solid is made when two liquids are mixed.

Product – the substance made in a chemical reaction.

Proton – a positively charged particle found in the nucleus of atoms.

Quadrat – a defined area used to sample a location.

Reactant – the substance at the start of a chemical reaction.

Receptor – the part of the nervous system that detects a stimulus.

Reflex action – a fast, automatic response.

Relative atomic mass – the average mass of an atom of an element compared to the twelfth of a carbon atom.

Relative formula mass – the sum of the atomic masses of all atoms in a molecule.

Resistance – the measure of how hard it is to get a current through a component at a particular potential difference / voltage.

Glossary of Key Words

Resultant force – the total force acting on an object (the effect of all the forces combined).

Risk – the danger (normally to health) associated with a procedure, action or event.

Speed–time graph – a graph showing speed against time taken; the gradient of the line represents acceleration.

Static electricity – a concentration of charge on an insulating material which is unable to move.

Stem cell – a cell of a human embryo or adult bone marrow that has the ability to differentiate.

Stimulus – a change in an organism's environment.

Synapse – a small gap between adjacent neurons.

Tissue – a collection of similar cells to carry out a function.

Titration – a method used to find the concentration of an acid or alkali.

Transect – a fixed path across an area of study.

Transformer – an electrical device used to change the potential difference / voltage of alternating currents.

Velocity – an object's speed and direction.

Voltage – a measurement of the potential difference between two points in a circuit.

Work done – work is done on a body or object when energy is transferred to it.

Yield – the amount of product obtained from a reaction.

Zygote – a cell formed by the fusion of the nuclei of a male sex cell and a female sex cell (gametes).

HT **Active site** – the place where the molecule fits into the enzyme.

Active transport – the movement of a substance against a concentration gradient.

Auxin – a plant hormone that affects the growth and development of a plant.

Chain reaction – a reaction, e.g. nuclear fission, that is self-sustaining.

Denatured enzyme – an enzyme that has had its shape destroyed and can no longer catalyse reactions.

Isotope – an atom of the same element that contains different numbers of neutrons.

Messenger RNA (mRNA) – the molecule that carries the genetic code out of the nucleus.

Nuclear fission – the splitting of atomic nuclei, which is accompanied by a release in energy.

Nuclear reactor – the place where fission takes place in a nuclear power station.

Therapeutic cloning – cloning a cell to make a healthy tissue to replace a damaged one.

Uranium – a radioactive element often used as nuclear fuel.

Velocity–time graph – a graph that shows how velocity (speed in a given direction) changes with time.

Key

| relative atomic mass |
| **atomic symbol** |
| name |
| atomic (proton) number |

| 1 | H hydrogen 1 |

Periodic Table

1	2												3	4	5	6	7	0
																		4 **He** helium 2
7 **Li** lithium 3	9 **Be** beryllium 4												11 **B** boron 5	12 **C** carbon 6	14 **N** nitrogen 7	16 **O** oxygen 8	19 **F** fluorine 9	20 **Ne** neon 10
23 **Na** sodium 11	24 **Mg** magnesium 12												27 **Al** aluminium 13	28 **Si** silicon 14	31 **P** phosphorus 15	32 **S** sulfur 16	35.5 **Cl** chlorine 17	40 **Ar** argon 18
39 **K** potassium 19	40 **Ca** calcium 20	45 **Sc** scandium 21	48 **Ti** titanium 22	51 **V** vanadium 23	52 **Cr** chromium 24	55 **Mn** manganese 25	56 **Fe** iron 26	59 **Co** cobalt 27	59 **Ni** nickel 28	63.5 **Cu** copper 29	65 **Zn** zinc 30		70 **Ga** gallium 31	73 **Ge** germanium 32	75 **As** arsenic 33	79 **Se** selenium 34	80 **Br** bromine 35	84 **Kr** krypton 36
85 **Rb** rubidium 37	88 **Sr** strontium 38	89 **Y** yttrium 39	91 **Zr** zirconium 40	93 **Nb** niobium 41	96 **Mo** molybdenum 42	[98] **Tc** technetium 43	101 **Ru** ruthenium 44	103 **Rh** rhodium 45	106 **Pd** palladium 46	108 **Ag** silver 47	112 **Cd** cadmium 48		115 **In** indium 49	119 **Sn** tin 50	122 **Sb** antimony 51	128 **Te** tellurium 52	127 **I** iodine 53	131 **Xe** xenon 54
133 **Cs** caesium 55	137 **Ba** barium 56	139 **La*** lanthanum 57	178 **Hf** hafnium 72	181 **Ta** tantalum 73	184 **W** tungsten 74	186 **Re** rhenium 75	190 **Os** osmium 76	192 **Ir** iridium 77	195 **Pt** platinum 78	197 **Au** gold 79	201 **Hg** mercury 80		204 **Tl** thallium 81	207 **Pb** lead 82	209 **Bi** bismuth 83	[209] **Po** polonium 84	[210] **At** astatine 85	[222] **Rn** radon 86
[223] **Fr** francium 87	[226] **Ra** radium 88	[227] **Ac*** actinium 89	[261] **Rf** rutherfordium 104	[262] **Db** dubnium 105	[266] **Sg** seaborgium 106	[264] **Bh** bohrium 107	[277] **Hs** hassium 108	[268] **Mt** meitnerium 109	[271] **Ds** darmstadtium 110	[272] **Rg** roentgenium 111								

Elements with atomic numbers 112–116 have been reported but not fully authenticated

*The lanthanoids (atomic numbers 58–71) and the actinoids (atomic numbers 90–103) have been omitted.

The relative atomic masses of copper and chlorine have not been rounded to the nearest whole number.

Data Sheet

Tests for Positively Charged Ions

Ion	Test	Observation
Calcium Ca^{2+}	Add dilute sodium hydroxide	A white precipitate forms; the precipitate does not dissolve in excess sodium hydroxide
Copper Cu^{2+}	Add dilute sodium hydroxide	A light blue precipitate forms; the precipitate does not dissolve in excess sodium hydroxide
Iron(II) Fe^{2+}	Add dilute sodium hydroxide	A green precipitate forms; the precipitate does not dissolve in excess sodium hydroxide
Iron(III) Fe^{3+}	Add dilute sodium hydroxide	A red-brown precipitate forms; the precipitate does not dissolve in excess sodium hydroxide
Zinc Zn^{2+}	Add dilute sodium hydroxide	A white precipitate forms; the precipitate dissolves in excess sodium hydroxide

Tests for Negatively Charged Ions

Ion	Test	Observation
Carbonate CO_3^{2-}	Add dilute acid	The solution effervesces; carbon dioxide gas is produced (the gas turns limewater from colourless to milky)
Chloride Cl^-	Add dilute nitric acid, then add silver nitrate	A white precipitate forms
Bromide Br^-	Add dilute nitric acid, then add silver nitrate	A cream precipitate forms
Iodide I^-	Add dilute nitric acid, then add silver nitrate	A yellow precipitate forms
Sulfate SO_4^{2-}	Add dilute nitric acid, then add barium chloride or barium nitrate	A white precipitate forms

Index

Index